# Reflections
# For
# Burden Bearers

## Eric H Janzen

Reflections for Burden Bearers
Copyright © 2019 Eric H Janzen

All rights reserved. No part of this publication may be reproduced, stored in a retrieval system, or transmitted in any form by any means—electronic, mechanical, photocopying, recording, or otherwise—except for brief quotations for purpose of reviews or schoolwork, without the prior written permission of the author.

To contact the author: ehj1@telus.net

## Dedication

This book is dedicated to the many people who have attended Samuel's Mantle over the years and graciously listened to me teach from time to time about burden bearing and listening to Jesus.

# Contents

Dedication ............................................................................. i

Introduction ........................................................................ iii

One     A Stairway before Me ................................................ 1

Two     God Will Meet You On the Dark Waters ................. 7

Three    Love, Submission, and Transformation .................. 16

Four     Mercy-Love ............................................................... 23

Five      Rest Meets Rest ........................................................ 34

Six       The Light of the World ........................................... 42

Seven    A Revealed Gift ........................................................ 52

Eight     Sin, Your Eyes, and Seeing God ............................. 57

Nine     Faith in Crisis ........................................................... 67

Ten      The Dark Night of the *What!?* ............................ 74

Conclusion ....................................................................... 100

# Introduction

After writing *A Handbook for Burden Bearers*, I had the idea that I should write some kind of a devotional for spiritually sensitive burden bearing people. However, as I tried to work on the idea it proved to be incredibly frustrating. As I pondered why I was having so much difficulty, I eventually did what I try to teach people to do: I prayed about it. The Lord asked me why I was ignoring what I'd already written at various times over the last few years. I began to realize that it was more than likely that themes I often reflect on and think about in my own spiritual life are the kind of themes others like me would probably identify with. In this book, you will find ten reflections I've written based on some of my experiences with Jesus. They each touch on recurring themes of the challenges and the joys of the spiritual life. Spiritually sensitive people share in some common struggles because of their gifting. My hope is that in some of these, rather personal, reflections readers will find helpful insights and teaching that will encourage them in their own lives. It is somewhat daunting to share with others what are in actuality glimpses into my personal life, but I believe such vulnerability is worth it even if only a few find something beneficial within these writings.

If you aren't a burden bearer or spiritually sensitive, I think you will still find something of value in these reflections, so please don't let labels keep you from reading them. I feel a certain kinship with spiritually sensitive Christians wherever they may be, but I also write for all who want to know and follow Jesus with depth and an open heart.

Each reflection ends with a prayer I've written. These are meant as aids for your own prayers. Sometimes we need a jumping off point to help us. Feel free to pray them as written or use them as a framework for your own. Usually, once we begin praying, our own words begin to flow. There are also a few bits of poetry throughout the book. I wrote these as well…samplings from my journal. I hope you enjoy them.

I want to invite anyone who reads this book to send any questions you have to me. I love questions. I believe they are the best way to learn. I always learn something when people ask me a question about what I think or have experienced because the process allows me to examine them that much more.

May the following pages bless you, challenge you, but most of all give you some hope for the journey.

*Radiant feet on*
*Steps under moonlight rise like*
*Mist atop dark water*

*Golden light frames our*
*Table as we speak of the*
*Quiet heart and fire*

# One
## A Stairway before Me

On a pleasant spring day one May, I was walking home from work. It was sunny, warmer than usual, but perfect walking weather. As I left work, I began to pray. This is the main reason I walk home from work. I enjoy visiting with Jesus as I make my way home.

On this particular day, as I began to pray, the eyes of my heart saw a stairway before me. It moved with me as I walked, always in front of me. At first it was very plain looking, just a white outline of a stairway. The steps were wide and went upward. I could see six of them before the rest were lost to my sight. I decided to ask the Lord about it, since he seemed to be showing this to me. He invited me to ask him questions, so I began with a simple one.

"Lord, what are these stairs meant to represent?"

Immediately, I sensed that they were symbolic of my heart connection with Him. Not only this, it represented my connection to the spiritual realm around me and in the heavenly realms.

"Lord, if you could give these stairs a color, what color would you choose?" I asked next.

The stairway took on two hues of blue. One was navy blue and the other was brighter, like aqua blue. I was surprised by the two different shades and I asked him why he showed me this.

*"The navy blue represents the flow of deeper revelation happening in your heart. You aren't always aware in your mind of the conversation occurring in your heart—spirit to Spirit. What happens in that flow rises up when you are ready to contemplate it with your mind, but see the seeds and the roots of what I am teaching you are already taking place within you. The lighter blue is the flow of your prophetic gifting and all that is involved with that—when you listen and minister to others this is the revelation flowing between us."*

After He said this, the stairway looked more like a stream of water flowing down steps and I understood there was this flow happening between my heart and God's heart. It was amazing to see it in such a visual way.

I have been in a season of learning to look and see with the eyes of my heart, so I asked the Lord if there were any angels attached to this stairway. I then saw two angels standing to either side at the base of the steps...so right in front of me. It was so vivid at first, I felt awkward being so close to them. I wondered how I couldn't have noticed them right away. They were the kind of angels I'm used to seeing—serious and focused on their task. I asked the Lord if they went up and down the stairway like the angels Jacob saw at the Bethel ladder. His answer surprised me.

*"No, these angels stand guard over this place in the spirit. You have opened yourself to me without reservation, which is to be commended, but it also makes you vulnerable in the spiritual realms, so I set angels to guard your connection to the heavenly realms. They are there to ensure unclean spirits do not take advantage of your openness."*

I felt such gratitude that the Lord would take care of me like that. I'm somewhat tentative when it comes to interacting with any kind of spirit that isn't Holy Spirit, but I asked the

Lord if I could say a thank you to the angels for their work. He said yes, so I simply nodded to them and said, "Thank you for watching over me. I really appreciate it." I could sense a warmth in response... a genuine feeling of care, as though they were saying, "We are glad to do it."

Next, the Lord prompted me by saying, *"Why not ask about how this flow can be affected?"*

"Well, I imagine worship is one way," I responded. "What happens to the flow if I spend time worshipping you?" This is what I did. I began to worship God in my heart with simple prayers of gratitude for who He is.

"I thank you Abba for your love for me. I thank you for your mercy. You are so kind. You are so generous. You are so patient and so faithful. Thank you for loving me and helping me when I struggle..." You get the idea. After a few minutes of worshipping, I looked closely at the stairway and the flow had indeed changed. I noticed that the aqua blue color had increased in amount. The navy blue was still there...as much as before, but now there was also more of the other hue.

*"When you worship, you enter into a deeper place with my Presence,"* the Lord whispered. *"Then the flow increases...your gifting, whatever someone's gifting is, will always function at a deeper and more powerful level when it is from a heart of worship...true worship."*

The Lord and I went on to discuss worshipping in spirit and truth. When we worship God genuinely from the heart (spirit), that deepest place of our being, our connection with him flows freely. Out of that deep worship, we can experience so much more of Jesus Christ and his kingdom. Worshipping in spirit and truth shows us that we are the temple of the Holy Spirit and it draws us into his presence where we are humbled. In this kind of worship, we set aside our opinions, our paradigms, our 'certainties', and we acknowledge the Lordship of Jesus...all we can do is be filled by the vision of his love, grace, mercy, and hope. We lift *him* up and begin to lose sight of ourselves just as Paul wrote...we decrease so that Jesus may increase. This is the worship of intimacy and it leads us into an ever-deepening friendship with Jesus...a friendship founded in the reverence we have for his immense love for us. This conversation is ongoing, but that's a snapshot of what we were talking about on that day.

The other activity that increases this flow is prayer. It seems too obvious to say, but the conversations we have with God keep us connected with him in the Spirit. As we pray, we position ourselves before God. We face him, we see him, and we are drawn into his presence and atmosphere. The more we speak to him and listen for his voice, the more we get to know him. If you want to know God, to have a deep relationship with him, then talk to him. I realized as I was walking and contemplating this stairway before me, that it was indeed in the context of prayer that all of this revelation had happened...I set out to visit with Jesus...in short, I prayed.

"What else can increase this flow between my heart and your heart, between this realm and the heavenly realms?" I asked.

*"Reading my Word can also increase this flow, but it must be with an open heart, just as it is with worship and prayer,"* the Lord replied.

This is a tough one, especially if you've grown up in church or studied theology as I have. We tend to read the Bible according to a pattern we've learned over time. We come to familiar passages and, without thinking, apply the meaning we learnt years ago instead of being open to Holy Spirit's voice. What might he say about a passage that is different? Are we open to seeing something we've never noticed before? I had to pray and ask for that kind of openness.

I arrived home, feeling as though the hour-long walk had only been about half that. I thanked the Lord for such a great time. The result has been that I have become much more aware of the flow in my heart. I find that I can see that stairway whenever I look for it. I am learning to observe the movement with the eyes of my heart. My faith has been deepened and my hope for a growing connection with God has increased.

What is the lesson then? When we are willing to open our hearts—our inner being—to God, we allow a connection to form between Him and us. The relationship and experience we have with Jesus can ebb and flow depending on our choices and our actions. We can choose to neglect this spiritual connection and just go through the motions, which will leave us in a shallow relationship with God. On the other hand, we can choose to engage with Holy Spirit and care for the flow in our hearts. If we picture this connection as a stream, we are looking for ways to keep the stream from becoming clogged with obstacles restricting the flow. We are looking for signs that the stream's level is going down...drying up, so to speak. The ways we increase the flow of our connection with God are through an open heart first, trusting in his love, faithfulness and goodness. As we begin to know who God is, our worship, prayer, and study not only keeps our heart connection vibrant, but also increases it.

ERIC H JANZEN
## Prayer

*Father, I thank you for your love for me. I thank you for your invitation to be connected to you—heart to heart. I open my deep heart to you and ask that you would fill my spirit with your Spirit. I pray that the flow between us in the spiritual realm would be open and would increase. I trust you Lord Jesus and welcome your presence. Come and speak with me, showing me more of who you are, for I desire to both know you and follow you. Whatever obstacles may be in the way of our connection, I pray that you would remove them. Show me, God, what I need to let go of so that more of your presence can fill my heart. Lord, I pray that you would help me to overcome whatever may be causing our relationship to decrease. I choose to worship you, Jesus. I choose to offer you prayer from an open heart. I choose to hear your Word with open ears, listening for the voice of your Spirit—Amen.*

**Scripture for Reflection:**
2 Kings 3:9-16
1 Samuel 10:5-7
Luke 24:13-35
Acts 8:26-40

## Two
## God Will Meet You
## on the Dark Waters

In February of 2016, I had a dream. In this dream, I was climbing a mountain at night. The mountain had a zigzag path leading to its summit, but the hike was still difficult. My legs grew heavy as the muscles got heavier and heavier. At last, I reached the top of the mountain and stepped onto a plateau instead of a peak. Before me, I saw a curving, white sandy beach glowing under moon and starlight. A grassy hill overlooked this beach and I could see some other figures in the distance near some park benches. From the beach, a vast dark ocean stretched to the far horizon where I could see a great, white light glowing in the night. I walked down to the beach and thought about how strange it was to have found an ocean at the top of a mountain. As I sat down in the sand, I felt a deep peace come over me….and I woke up. I knew immediately this was a dream that would remain important to me for a long time.

Since having this dream, I have used the very end as a meeting place with Jesus for prayer and contemplation. It is a picture that brings me to peace and allows me to enter into God's restful presence. I think I know what the dream means, but have always felt it was deeper than I knew. This is the way of dreams sometimes.

In November 2018, some two years after having this dream, a remarkable thing occurred—at least remarkable to me. I was at church, singing as best I could during the worship time. I have been learning to connect with God from the heart during prayer. Recently, I have been attempting to worship him from that deep place of the spirit as well. I found myself drawn into silence as Holy Spirit drew very near and a heavy peace came over me. I felt like the world around me became a dull noise as my inner vision filled with a beach and an ocean. Slowly, the dream began to play out around me once more. This was remarkable to me because I didn't initiate it as a meeting place. I was aware that Holy Spirit was bringing me into this particular dream, but now as a vision (for those who care about such distinctions). I looked around and all was familiar. It was exactly as I remembered the dream…the sand was the same, the moon and the stars were the same, and the bright light on the horizon of this strange mountaintop ocean remained. I could feel the love and peace of God's presence all around me.

"I love this place," I whispered in my heart.

*"You are not meant to camp here and do nothing,"* I heard the Lord whisper back.

"What do you mean?" I said.

Then as though they'd been there the whole time, I saw other people on the beach. In the water there were small wooden boats floating near the shore.

"What are they doing here?" I wondered.

There weren't many people…maybe a dozen or so. I watched them closely because they were not having the same response to this place as I was. Instead, they looked around with questions on their faces. They looked at one another as people looking for directions do. Some people shrugged while others looked frustrated or even frightened.

I knew they were supposed to get into the boats and I encouraged them to do so, gesturing kindly towards them. They got into these boats and when they did, they began to float out onto the ocean, moving towards the horizon where the great light shines, only they looked apprehensive, unsure of what was happening. My heart went out to them and I heard Holy Spirit say, *"Tell them, God will meet them on the dark waters."* I did this and when I spoke those words, I saw Jesus appear in every boat with each of them, a white light surrounding him and them. Not only was I comforted by this amazing sight, I could easily see that for each of these people it was exactly what they needed as they moved forward on their journey with Jesus. After this, the vision ended and I found myself back in church wondering what had just happened to me. What was the Lord saying?

When we find ourselves hearing from Jesus, we do well to begin with ourselves as the one needing the message. Sometimes, I feel like I've been sailing on dark waters for my entire life. We each have our own struggles, whether they are internal or external stresses. We all experience suffering in some way and in our suffering we often know what it is like to feel alone and in darkness. For some there are lifelong struggles that never seem to go away. I have endured this kind of struggle for many years and I often wonder if I will ever be free from it. Such an admission is frightening, but I think far more of us carry such a burden than we know. From depression to anxiety, to fear and uncontrollable anger, addictions to self-doubt etc…we can all probably point to something in our lives we wish could be removed, healed, or at least controlled a little better. There are events in some of our lives we absolutely wish we could go back in time and prevent. The reality is that all people find themselves on dark waters, feeling alone in a small boat, unsure of what to do or where they are going.

While the reasons may vary and are unique to our own stories, God is bringing a truth to light. The reason I can sit on the beach in my dream and find peace and rest is that I learned through a long, gruelling season of life, Jesus always meets with me. It doesn't matter how I feel or how horrible things are. When I look for him, I find him with me. This assurance didn't come without a struggle. The last thing I want to say to anyone is that it's easy to find God's presence when life is shrouded in darkness. In fact, it can be excruciating. Allowing our faith to stand up when all we feel is the crushing weight of circumstance and heartache is hard. I've written elsewhere about my experience of the dark night of the soul, the season in which I learned this truth, but more importantly experienced it. I wouldn't bother to share my dream and vision with you if I didn't know that what it shows me is true. This is why I can stand up on that beach and call out to others with what I know to be true: "God will meet you on the dark waters!" It's a sure promise. Yet, I've visited with many people who find this a difficult truth to believe.

It can be very difficult to see or feel the presence of Jesus when we are being overwhelmed. We need help. When I endured my dark night of the soul, there were times where I couldn't pray, I couldn't worship, I couldn't *do* anything spiritual. I recall lying on my bed often, desperately trying to muster up enough spiritual energy to connect with God and feeling utterly empty and alone. It was an incredibly difficult time in my life, a time of agony, anger, and darkness (you will read about this dark night of the soul later in this book.) However, when I look back on that time now, I see Jesus and myself together throughout the entire season. He was there. In fact, he was *always* there. When I couldn't pray, he was praying for me. When I couldn't worship, he was worshipping for me. When I was in agony and pain, he sat with me and endured every harsh word I had for him with compassion and love. When I could pray, but the words of my prayer were just words to my ears and nothing more, he filled them with his own prayer and brought my prayers to life. I couldn't see him in the midst of it. I couldn't feel him or hear him clearly…unless I was praying for other people (oh that drove me crazy!) When my season in the dark night began to shift and change, I began to see how Jesus had taken every step through it with me. This time in my life changed me. It taught me by experience the truth that David wrote about in Psalm 139:7-12 (please forgive the lengthy quote):

*Where could I go from your Spirit,*
*or flee from Your face?*
*If I should ascend into heaven, You*
*would be there;*
*If I should descend into Hades, You*
*would be there;*
*If I should take up my wings at dawn*
*And pitch camp at the furthest part of the sea,*
*Even there Your hand would lead me,*
*And Your right hand would hold me.*
*And I said, 'Perhaps darkness shall*
*cover me,'*
*But the night shall be light to my*
*delight;*
*For darkness shall not be dark*
*because of You,*
*And the night shall be bright as day;*
*As its darkness, so also shall be its*
*light.*

We all come to a time in our lives where we reach a shore looking out at what seems to be darkness. Our knees may grow weak with fear. Our hearts may be overcome with anger and we ask questions for which we can find no answers that satisfy. We may lament or form a fist and shake it in frustration. All of this is fine. All of this is normal…yet this shore is not where you have to stop. David paints an amazing word picture in Psalm 139, one I find both comforting and now familiar. When he thinks the darkness will cover him, the night is lit up. Why? The darkness will not be dark because of God's presence…he who is the light will make all of that darkness into light.

On the dark waters, Jesus meets with us. In my vision, his presence brought light with it into each of those boats, so that each of those people could see and hear…and feel the presence of Jesus with them in the way they could connect with him. There is no formula for this connection. Your heart is different from mine and your experience is different. Yet, there is one common truth available to all of us. A truth, I want to share with you if you find yourself on the dark waters in your spirit: Jesus will not only meet with you on the dark waters, he is *already there* with you. It may take some time for you to be able to see him, to hear him, and to feel him, but I know that he is there.

If you're willing, close your eyes and picture a beach at night. Now picture yourself in a small, two-person boat floating gently on the water. There are stars above you…angels covering you while you journey. There is a bright moon lighting the water…it isn't total darkness. Now, picture a blond haired man in his forty's with a slightly greying beard standing on the shore (that's me!). I'm pointing at your boat, just a brother who's been where you are on the dark waters.

"Look! There he is! Jesus is standing in your boat!" Now let his light and his love, and his life surround you.

## REFLECTIONS FOR BURDEN BEARERS

We need to have some hope in these days. I'm hoping you'll find the strength not to give up. Don't take my word for it, but test the waters, so to speak. Hold on to the hem of his garment, don't let go. Jesus told us we would have troubles in this world. We know dark waters will come, but you should know dark waters will also go. Jesus is with us before they ever come into our lives, he is with us every step of the way as we navigate them, and he is with us when we reach the other side of them. Take heart! Jesus has overcome the darkness, as David wrote:

*"For darkness shall not be dark*
*because of You,*
*And the night shall be bright as day;*
*As its darkness, so also shall be its light."*

ERIC H JANZEN
## Prayer

*Father, I thank you for your presence. I thank you for your compassion. Lord, Jesus I pray that you would draw near to me when I find myself in darkness of heart and mind. Lord, sometimes life is overwhelming. Sometimes the pain in my heart is too much and I feel like I can't go on. In these times, Lord, I pray that you would sit with me and embrace my heart in your loving arms. Lord, I choose to trust that you are with me even if my emotions and my mind can't perceive your loving presence. I choose to believe by faith that you are here with me. Lord, I thank you that you don't make light of my burdens or my pain, but show me compassion and mercy. Thank you for your love. When my worship and my prayer feel empty, lend me your very own. I thank you Holy Spirit for your friendship and thank you for sharing your own voice with mine. Jesus, help me to remember that you love me for who I am. There is nothing I have to do to earn your love. Thank you for receiving me and loving me without hesitation even when I find myself in dark waters—Amen.*

**Scripture for Reflection:**
Psalm 139
Luke 22:39-46
Romans 8:26-39
Mark 4:35-41

So come run with me
Through desert valleys
And up mountains high
Sail atop seas under
Storming skies
I've got a hand
That won't let go

So come rest your head on me
When you feel blind
And just can't see
When fear tries to break you apart
Ease your heart and know
I've got a heart
That won't let go

Put your hand in my hand
Put your heart in my heart
I won't let go

# Three
# Love, Submission, and Transformation

The love of Jesus Christ elevates us to a place in the Spirit where we begin to be healed. As we are healed, our ability to experience who God is deepens. That is to say, we begin to experience the goodness of God. The goodness of God is difficult to describe, for he is divine, so we use what language we can to attempt to create a picture of that divine goodness. We can say the goodness of God is kind, full of grace, merciful, peaceful, restful, and gentle. We can say the goodness of God is powerful, joyful, accepting, strengthening, wise, and full of love. We can say even more than this, yet each word we use fails, at some point, in fully expressing these attributes of God. For example, when I say God is kind, I fail to fully express or describe for you just how kind he truly is. His kindness goes so far beyond what you or I can conceive. Eventually, his kindness will offend us. For God, who is love, is able to show complete kindness to those we cannot—those we would consider deserving of wrath and rage, vengeance and punishment. We shouldn't despair when this happens, but be grateful. In moments where we see clearly the ways we are not yet like Jesus, we find the opportunity to open our heart to his love, his Spirit, and his deeper transformation.

As Christians, we don't speak enough of this transformation, this hope in the grace to be changed into people whose hearts reflect the heart of Jesus. Instead, we have focused on points of theology and moral regulation. We are caught up in questions that lead us down paths away from Jesus, away from our Father, and away from our dearest companion, Holy Spirit. We are not meant to control the world—we are meant to be those who bear the Spirit of Christ within the world, reflecting the goodness of God and pointing to Jesus Christ. As bearers of the Spirit, we should be reflecting the goodness of God, as described above in its limited way, to all people. How can we transform the world if we ourselves refuse to be transformed by who Jesus is? Words are meaningless when the heart has not grasped what we speak with our mouths.

Jesus was so wise. He knew how we would live and warned us about the risks we would face in our wending ways. One of the wisest teachings he gave us is the metaphor of the tree and its fruit. We can always examine what is going on in our hearts by the fruit our actions, our ways of thinking, and our beliefs are producing. The simplest way to view it is this: Am I led to a deeper love for God? Am I led to a deeper love for people, for human beings, whom the Gospel reveals are all my neighbors? For those who hunger and thirst for a deeper experience of Jesus Christ, and the presence of his kingdom, there must be a renewed commitment to the transformation of the spirit. We must turn away from anything we recognize as an obstacle keeping us from submitting to Jesus. As the proverb says, *'...in all your ways submit to him, and he will make your path straight....'*

How do we pursue this grace of transformation? How do we become people who submit to Jesus? Submission is such an alien word to the western mind. It has been made almost completely negative, yet Jesus told us that those who will lose their life will find it in him. Jesus is our life. To submit all our ways to him, is not to enter into some kind of dull and boring existence. On the contrary, it is the gate through which we enter a straight path traveled with the most interesting and amazing person ever—God! We must learn to remain in the place where we receive God's love. With open hearts, we discover the key to ongoing transformation. With an open heart, we begin to experience both a deeper connection to God and a deeper friendship with Jesus. This is why Jesus teaches us to abide in him. John 15 is worth reading in its entirety on this point, but consider even these few words, *"If you abide in me, and my words abide in you, you will ask what you desire, and it shall be done for you. By this my Father is glorified, that you bear much fruit; so you will be my disciples."* (John 15:7-8). We are invited to this abiding relationship with Jesus through his Spirit living in us.

What is it that we desire? I want you to consider the idea that what you desire is very important. The fruit of what you desire is very important. We could focus on a desire for power, expecting God to act in the way that we want. Yet, too often, the fruit of this kind of desire doesn't turn out very well. However, we could have desires that grow out of our submission to Jesus, desires that focus on becoming like him, being transformed so that we become those who reflect his goodness. Remaining in him, abiding and engaging with his presence living within the heart, allows us to experience a living and vibrant connection with him. This should be the desire we ask for. Imagine the fruit that grows within the heart when its first and foremost love, its first and foremost vision is Jesus. From such a heart, glory will come to the Father, for we would at least become possible signs of the presence of Jesus and his kingdom in the world. As such signs, we must look like and sound like the goodness of God as revealed to us by Jesus. That goodness comes alive within us, expressed through us, both spiritually and practically, as we abide and remain in our first love, Jesus Christ. The Holy Spirit then moves through us in exactly the right way at the right moment to display the love of God our Father to the world. Yet, to be such signs, we must submit in all our ways. How else can we keep in step with the Spirit? We have to know him and recognize him if we are to walk in step with him. This requires abiding humility and an open heart. We must become followers of Jesus, ready always to lay our egos and pride down (daily!) so that we as the bearers of his Holy Spirit act as true ambassadors of the kingdom of heaven. We must display the fruit of his presence. We must become the very expression of love, pouring out our lives for the sake of others, regardless of who they may be, just as Christ did for us and continues to do for us as he intercedes on our behalf before the Father.

Whatever draws you out of the place of God's love, will dull your spirit's ability to experience his goodness and his presence. Do you find yourself thinking of a particular person or group as your enemy? Hear the alarm bells ringing! Recall to mind the teachings of Jesus…love your enemy…forgive those who wrong you…pray for those who persecute you…. Do you find yourself growing numb, growing bitter? Hear the alarm bells ringing! Abide in Jesus, let his life fill your heart…you are meant for abundant life. Do you find yourself judging others? Judging the society around you and the anger, and even rage, that accompanies all that judging? Hear the alarm bells ringing! You are being drawn out of the place of abiding with Jesus, out of his transcending gift of peace…and worse, you are being pulled away from Christ's core commandment: love God and love your neighbour. As the Apostle John wrote for us, "*Whoever confesses that Jesus is the Son of God, God abides in him, and he in God. And we have known and believed the love that God has for us. God is love, and he who abides in love abides in God, and God in him.*" (1 John 4:15-16). If the fruit of our heart and our thinking is not leading us to an ever-deepening ability to love, then we must stop and examine our lives. Again, we shouldn't despair or be discouraged when we come to those moments. This is the moment of beautiful repentance. A moment where we can open our heart to the transformation of the Spirit, echoing Psalm 51…*create in me a clean heart and renew a right spirit within me*…. Then, our amazing God draws near. His love, the unrelenting love of Jesus, through his gentle mercy and grace, elevates us to a place in the Spirit as I said at the beginning. Here we are healed. Once more, the heart is softened, made malleable in the hands of a loving Father, whose goodness is unparalleled. We are accepted and the love of his Spirit draws our own spirit out of the shadow and fog, reawakening our hearts. He opens the eyes of the heart and heals our minds. We must learn this essential truth if we are to hope for the transformation he has promised us—that he has won for us. God's love for us is the most powerful foundation we can experience. It eclipses everything else we could possibly build the life of the heart on. If we have any desire or hope to grow in the Spirit, we must learn to abide and remain in our first and foremost love, Jesus Christ.

## Prayer

*Father, I thank you for your goodness. I am amazed at the depth of just how good you are. Words cannot fully express how loving, kind, gracious, and merciful you are. Words fall short in describing how compassionate, patient, and faithful you are. Lord, when your Spirit shows me how I need to learn to love more deeply, give me the grace to hear what you are saying. I want to follow you Jesus and I want to be transformed a little more each day into your likeness. I humble my heart before you and today, Lord, I say that you are my first and foremost love. I submit all my ways to you. I choose to lay aside those things that draw me away from fixing my eyes on you and your great love for me and for my neighbor. Lord, fill my vision with you and you alone, for I want to be filled with your Spirit. Jesus, here is my open heart—I invite you to abide within me. Show me your goodness and create in me a clean heart that can reflect the glory of your goodness to others. Make me one who lives as an authentic invitation to the kingdom of heaven. When others look at me, Jesus I pray they would see and hear your open hands filled with the love of God for them—Amen.*

**Scripture for Reflection:**
Proverbs 3:5-6—Sit with these words and let them fill your heart. They are familiar to many of us, but the truth contained in these verses is profound. Make it a prayer you say daily.
2 Corinthians 3:12-17
Psalm 51
1 John 4:7-21

## ERIC H JANZEN

When the sun lights up
The window
And eyes open and close
My first thought is about you
As the sun rises further
Casting a shadow on the wall
And eyes stay open
My first words are for you
Thank you for loving me
Thank you for befriending me
Without you
I don't know who I would be
As the sun sets
My last thoughts
My last words
Are for you
Thank you for loving me
Without you
I don't know who I would be

# Four
# Mercy-Love

In the Sermon on the Mount, Jesus begins with a list of blessings. Among these, we find a call to mercy coupled with a promise: *Joyful are the merciful, for they shall be rejoicing daily in the mercy they receive.* Mercy is important—perhaps, more important than many realize. Mercy is at the core of the Gospel, grasping hands with love. Gospel mercy is the expression of God's love revealed to us through Jesus. When we lose sight of mercy's central place in our faith, we find ourselves in danger of no longer understanding Jesus, the cross, and the resurrection. Mercy is so powerful that within it is contained the power to change the world. It altered the course of human history as it was displayed in Christ's ministry, death, and resurrection.

Jesus didn't raise a new, unheard of theme when he pronounced the blessing in the Sermon on the Mount. Mercy is a theme running like a river through history. From the moment of the Fall right up to today, God has been on a mission of mercy. Throughout the Bible, we find God reaching out in compassion and kindness to a violent, unjust, and angry world. A world in decay because of sin needs mercy to move it towards life and healing. Mercy is more than some benevolent concept…it is more than good, optional advice. For the follower of Jesus, mercy is a way of living and a way of being. Lest we be careless, let us also admit this: *mercy is not easy*.

In John 8:34-36, Jesus makes an incredibly powerful statement. He tells his listeners that everyone who sins is a slave to Sin. They are a slave to a power holding sway over them. Slaves, Jesus notes, have no real place in a family…they do not genuinely belong to it. However, one who is born to the family belongs to it forever. Then he says: 'So, if the Son sets you free you will be free indeed.' What an incredible message. Those who are slaves to Sin can only be set free from that slavery by the One who has the authority to do so. Jesus is that Son with the authority to set us free from our slavery to Sin. Jesus brings a message of hope…of freedom from the twisting corruption of the Fall and all the decay it has sown into the world—both spiritually and physically. His action is centred on freeing us, and he promises us that this is true freedom. No longer slaves, we are adopted into the family as full children. The New Testament writers will expand on this understanding of freedom after Jesus has ascended. It is important. The lives we live with Jesus depend on this freedom. In the language of my youth, we used to talk about moving from the kingdom of darkness into the kingdom of heaven…the old Self becoming a new creation…and—dare we say it—being born again. What is important to see is that when we follow Jesus, giving our spirits to his, we are set free from the dominating power of Sin. As Paul says, we are no longer slaves to Sin but are filled with Holy Spirit by whom we call out to God: Dad! Father! We are drawn out of an existence of enmity and separation from God into a place of remarkable relationship as both reverent worshippers and close friends with the living God.

Now what does all that have to do with mercy? The freedom that Jesus wins for us and imparts to us *is* mercy. It effects change on both the grandest scale and on the most intimate level. We say that Jesus has overcome Death and Sin, the powers that held sway over humanity, dethroning them at the cross and utterly defeating them when he rose to life and left the tomb. Jesus has set us free (free indeed!) from their power and is leading us into his kingdom. Paul gives a great picture of this in Ephesians 4:8 where he quotes from Psalm 68, *"When he ascended on high, he led captives (slaves, prisoners) in his train and gave gifts to men."* In the Psalm, men give gifts to God, but Paul reverses it here showing his listeners the fullness of God's grace and mercy through Jesus towards them. God is pulling us up to his place, his home, his Way of being, and giving us all we need to do so…all through his Son.

The freedom of Jesus touches us in the most private depths of our hearts. When we open our spirit to Jesus, receiving his salvation, we enter a new reality. In this new reality all the power of Jesus' freedom action at the cross and in his resurrection, takes root within us by the presence of Holy Spirit. Those things that have enslaved us now must contend with—and submit to—the transforming power and presence of Jesus. They are passing away as the life of Jesus is filling us, changing us, and setting us free.

Jesus makes the point in John 8:34-36 that someone who is enslaved needs a power coming from the outside to set them free from that slavery. We need someone to step in on our behalf, someone who has the authority capable of truly breaking our bonds. This is what Jesus has done and is still doing for us.

In the book of the prophet Micah there is a verse, a very instructive verse, *"He has showed you, oh man, what is good. And what does the Lord require of you? To act justly and to love mercy and to walk humbly with your God."* (Micah 6:8). Through Micah, God expresses what he wants from people who say they love him and follow his ways. We see that mercy is not an afterthought, but rather at the centre of God's own values. What is interesting to note is that the Hebrew word used for mercy in this verse means something more like 'loyal love'. It describes the kind of love that God has shown for his people. This quality of love continues even in the face of betrayal and rebellion. This love doesn't give up even when those being loved spurn it completely. This is the covenant love of God. It shows mercy where punishment would be expected. It shows forgiveness where vengeance could be justified. In Micah, God calls his people to emulate that same incredibly powerful and deep love. God has been showing this mercy-love since the Fall when he mercifully removed Adam and Eve from Eden before they could eat from the tree of life. He showed mercy-love to Cain the first murderer. He showed mercy-love to Israel when they betrayed him and worshipped the Golden Calf. Though Jonah didn't approve, God showed mercy-love to repentant Nineveh. The examples of his mercy-love go on and on weaving through a dark human history refusing to embrace this kind of love. Yet, God never gives up…that is the essence of his mercy-love…it will not fail even in the face of the harshest and darkest rejection. When Micah tells his hearers that they are to love and be merciful in the same way, it is the highest calling—and incredibly challenging. Religious observance isn't what God wants from his people. Rather, he is looking for those who will join him in living according to his Ways. He wants us to become like him…those who will love even in the face of evil and abandonment.

In Jesus, all the mercy-love of God is exerted on our behalf. Jesus becomes our mercy on the cross. There where he is killed, unjustly punished, he prays, *'Father, forgive them for they know not what they do.'* These are perhaps the most important words ever uttered. They are the merciful declaration of God, his pronouncement over humanity—forgive them—let mercy-love answer their sin. Jesus freely chose mercy over punishment. Would he not have been justified in doing the opposite? If he'd called down a heavenly fire and spoke against his enemies, judging and destroying them, he would have done so with every right…at least from a human perspective. Yet, this is not his Way, this is not the heart of God, who is love and mercy. To avenge himself on us with violent retribution would have been to eat of the fruit, to partake in the twisting corruption of the Fall. God could not—would not—choose enmity in this way. It isn't in his nature to do so. He is at his very core, love, and love, we have discovered, forgives. It chooses mercy-love over judgment. It seeks reconciliation over vengeance. It prays for enemies and persecutors. It even shows mercy when it is horribly and diabolically wronged. Jesus' commitment to mercy should amaze us. It should make us stop in our tracks and ask why mercy is so important. What did Jesus understand and believe about mercy and forgiveness that we should be trying to understand ourselves?

We've made our way back to the blessing in the Sermon on the Mount and the challenge/promise contained within it. Jesus tells us if we are merciful—those who live out mercy-love—we will be shown mercy. Not only that, but we will be filled with joy as a result. Showing mercy when we have suffered is not to be trivialized. As I've said already, this is not easy. This is where spiritual depth meets what is perhaps its most difficult challenge. To choose forgiveness and mercy when we have been sinned against is—simply put—hard.

As I contemplated mercy, I saw a picture in my spirit. I saw myself standing in front of a tall mirror looking myself up and down. I heard Jesus say, *'Mercy is a mirror.'* I frowned in the mirror and thought to myself, 'Now what does that mean?' As I pondered this brief vision, I began to understand something about being merciful. Mercy requires us to enter to an uncomfortable vulnerability, a self-awareness that will show us aspects of our lives and ourselves we may not enjoy seeing. I slowly began to realize that it was in recognizing my own need for mercy that I would find the capacity to be merciful. To put it another way, when I grasp the mercy I've been shown, I am filled with joy (and relief!). God's Way is to realize that this means we shouldn't withhold that same mercy from others…he wants us to not only receive mercy from him and the joy inherent within it, but to then reflect that same Way in our lives, in who we are, emulating his character. We reflect God's reality and character when we act as he does. In choosing mercy-love, we reveal the character and presence of Jesus in this world of darkness and decay, where his light and his Way are so desperately needed. Love recognizes the good done to it and chooses to give away that same good. Mercy liberates. Recall Jesus' words, 'So if the Son sets you free, you will be free indeed.'

If God's Way is mercy-love, then the opposite response of withholding forgiveness and mercy is the way of Sin…the way of decay and death. Jesus' mercy at the cross, his action in his death and resurrection, liberates us from the powers of Sin and Death, and all their consequences. Choosing mercy-love is to turn our backs on the Old Way of Sin and embrace the eternal Way of God. Mercy leads to freedom, spiritual life, and joy. If we look into the mirror of mercy, seeing our need for the reception of mercy, then turn away and choose the old path, we enter into the parable of the unmerciful servant. This is one of Jesus' most uncomfortable and challenging parables. The servant is shown incredible mercy by his master, the kind that washes through one's heart and body. When he turns around and withholds a smaller mercy in a savage and brutal manner, we should be shocked and profoundly disappointed. How could he be so unmoved by his own experience of mercy? He didn't look into the mirror and grasp the truth of the forgiveness he was shown. The result is that he ends up lacking the capacity to forgive. Instead, it seems like he thinks something like, 'Phew! I got away with it...but just barely!' He shows little regard for the mercy he actually received, giving it no value.

The unmerciful servant is called to account for his lack of mercy. It is a stern and frightening warning...and instructive. Jesus reveals something about mercy and forgiveness in this parable. It illustrates what happens when mercy is rejected, when forgiveness falls to the wayside. The consequences turn on the unmerciful servant as though his choice to refuse giving mercy blocks the mercy meant to be shown to him. I used to think the master in the story was God, but perhaps we are to understand the master as being a symbol for Mercy itself. Mercy is not isolated from justice. When the unmerciful servant refused to show mercy, he faced the justice required for that refusal. In a sense he rejected the mercy shown him when he rejected the choice to show mercy to another.

Think of it this way: choosing mercy and forgiveness for your enemy, for the one who has wronged you, is like taking the offense and turning it into a ball. You stand at the edge of a field, looking out at a distant horizon, and you throw that ball. It soars into the air, carried on a wind of mercy into the distance until it is gone, never to return. Healing follows that throw. Freedom takes root and grows within you. The echoes of pain diminish and the presence of Jesus begins to fill the space where the pain of the ball once sat. Now imagine balling up the same pain, that same offense, and choosing not to be merciful. Choosing not to forgive creates a wall before you in that field. The horizon is not in sight. When you throw that ball it will rebound and return to you, striking you in the heart. The pain remains. It is renewed with every angry, unmerciful throw. It will bruise. It will crush. It will enslave your spirit until only bitterness and rage are left to you. This is a powerful emotional loop. For some this choice is all that makes sense, for the very idea of forgiving the one who has hurt them is too much. Yet, it leaves them in a spiritually debilitated state. Jesus wants us to be free and he knows that true mercy and forgiveness will liberate us. He wants more for us than to be stuck in our anger at the hurt we've suffered, the injustice we've experienced, and the trauma visited upon us. He wants us to overcome, to be freed from the spiritual death the sin of others is causing in us. Counter to the long-standing human tendency towards vengeance and the cycle of pain it causes, he has shown us that mercy and forgiveness are the path to freedom and healing.

Sin is at the center of the evil in every human heart…it's been there since the Fall, twisting and corrupting. It is the one trauma common to us all. Yet it is not the true center or foundation of the human spirit. We were made out of love. My friend Steve Nolte puts it this way, "God's love is the deepest seed in every human heart." Unfortunately, many hearts are so overwhelmed by darkness, sin, suffering, pain, and trauma, that this seed is deeply buried. Mercy-love has the power to reach through the muck and the mire, clearing it away, and exposing that seed of God's love. Once we genuinely understand this mercy-love, it reaches out and can transform even the most lost and broken among us. This is what Jesus does. He seeks the lost to free them, to save them. He welcomes the prodigals home and celebrates them. He loves his enemies—even from the cross, he forgives them. Jesus saw that mercy-love and forgiveness would loose the bonds of sin and its consequences.

When we choose the Way of mercy-love, we choose to agree with Jesus that the cycle of Sin's influence needs to be broken. Revenge, violence, violent justice, judgments of rage and retaliation…none of these has served to overcome Sin in our world, to stop injustice and evil. True transformation flows from Calvary, from the action of mercy-love in Jesus on the cross. His action of love is the power emanating through history that can stop the cycle and overcome the power of sin.

Yet, we must embrace it…receive it. This is the hard part isn't it? When we have been hurt, traumatized, suffered evil at the hands of another, we don't want to pause and consider the spiritual condition of our heart or theirs. We want to hold them by the scruff of the neck over a bottomless pit and drop them in. We want justice…and often, if we're honest, we want revenge. Deep inside, every heart knows it will bring little satisfaction, but it is powerful…it satisfies for a moment. However, the truth is that choosing vengeance cripples us even if it punishes our offender…the cycle of sin continues, and our pain remains. It will leave us with bitterness, anger, self-righteousness…and deeply unsatisfied. The heart will simply churn, caught in the grasp of pain that cannot be healed and resolved through choosing not to forgive. The condition will become intolerable. It will destroy us from the inside out. It is the ball coming back at us like a brick in the face. It may bruise our enemy, our offender, but it will crush us. Withholding mercy-love prevents any hope of beginning the deep healing Jesus wants for us. It allows the pain we have suffered to become an oppressor all its own. It dominates us and dictates to us *who* we are and *how* we are.

The blessing of being merciful is found in the joy and freedom it brings into our inner being. Joy in the sense of strengthened hope in place of painful despair…freedom in the sense of ending our pain and trauma's power to oppress us. Choosing mercy-love is to enter into the process of forgiveness. This can be a long road…an ongoing process to be sure. Deep pain and suffering isn't to be forgotten as in the unwise adage 'forgive and forget' (ridiculous!) Rather, our pain and suffering need to be acknowledged. Jesus always acknowledges our pain, our hurt, and our deepest traumas. He enters into them with us without hesitation and weeps with us in the place of our worst pain. He promises comfort for those who are caught in grief. Simply erasing our pain and painting smiles on our faces would be an act of denial, but that can never lead to healing. Denial in this way diminishes us, devalues us, because what has been done to us does matter. True justice acknowledges the wrongs done to us.

Jesus enters into our pain when we let him in and begins a real, powerful, and genuine work of healing. He comes alongside us and grieves with us. He isn't afraid to sit with us in our anger and our bitterness. He isn't afraid of our desire for revenge. He isn't afraid to partake in our suffering…he did this on the cross. Yet, he will gently call us to his Way of mercy-love. He will call us to the much deeper way of being he has shown us, because he wants true healing and freedom for us. His mercy-love is what can lead us towards freedom; lead us on a path of impossible mercy for the ones who have hurt us. He offers a way of freedom that overcomes the power of our pain over us. When we allow him to enter our pain with us, we will begin to see that bitterness, rage, despair…all the choking power of our pain can be overcome. The choice is admittedly difficult, but the path leads us into the freedom of the Son.

## REFLECTIONS FOR BURDEN BEARERS
## Prayer

*Father, I thank you for your mercy and your love. I am in awe of the depth of your commitment to love—you never stop loving and you never give up on loving us, even when in our own eyes we think you might. I ask Lord Jesus that you would fill my heart with your mercy-love and fill my heart with the joy you promised. Help me to understand the depth of mercy you have shown me and allow it be a treasure in my mind and my spirit, so that I will not hesitate to follow your way of mercy. Lord, I'm thankful you see my pain and that you don't take it lightly. I pray that you would give me the strength to forgive, for I want to choose your Way of mercy-love so that I can live in the freedom you want to release in my life. Lord Jesus, I pray that you would help me to see what you have for me beyond my pain. I want to enter into your will for me and be free from all that would hold me back—even my own unwillingness to let some hurts go. You are so kind to recognize that this isn't easy for me. You are so generous to help me take the steps forward towards forgiveness and mercy. Through the process of forgiveness, I pray that I would know you better and that our friendship would deepen—Amen.*

**Scripture for Reflection:**
Matthew 5:1-12—Reading the entire Sermon on the Mount is also an excellent idea.
Micah 6:1-8
Matthew 18:21-35
Psalm 32
Luke 15:11-32

# Five
## Rest Meets Rest

There is a theme running throughout the Bible that centers on the idea of rest and peace. If I use the term 'inner peace', many of us will very quickly think of something other than our faith in Jesus. We may think of new age people, or a meditating Buddhist, or maybe a yoga class…the idea of 'inner peace' is a broad one and a common pursuit around the world. There is angst in all of us, a lack of peace and rest in our very spirits to which we attempt to apply different answers and remedies. The idea that Jesus leads us to a place of inner peace is often treated as secondary as we move forward in our walk with him. Yet, for many of us, what drew us to God through Jesus was an experience of his peaceful touch on our hearts. When we first encounter his presence, it is the peace that his love brings which overwhelms us, a peace we continue to thirst for.

I can't tell you how thankful I am for the rest and peace of God. It has become the foundation for my daily life. I struggle every day to find that place of peace in the Spirit. Some days, I don't get there, but I am having the joy of finding that place more and more. What a joy to have learned that God has called us to be people of rest and peace. If you don't know that, then I have good news for you. God desires that you have inner peace. What is it like? How can one describe it?

It is like falling backwards into someone's arms...they catch you and hold you when your own strength has given way.

It is like not being able to breathe and suddenly your lungs open up and air rushes in.

It is like a pause button on the spinning world around you—or rather, it is as if you are paused while the world spins on, but you are no longer caught in its frantic flight.

It is like standing on a beach at the ocean's edge while the sun is setting and a perfect wind comes off the water surrounding you with a warm embrace as the evening air slightly chills you...and when you look to your side there is Jesus standing with you...smiling...it is well...it is well with my soul.

Here is the difference we encounter: our inner peace isn't based on methods of breathing, or rituals, or mantras, or in wearing the right crystals or jewellery. Instead, our peace is found *in a person*, in the presence of Jesus. We are learning to abide—to live with and remain in his presence. This is the place of grace. This is the experience of the empowering presence flowing to us, providing us with strength that is not our own. He instills in us peace that is greater than our anxiety and rest that is greater than our exhaustion.

His presence produces a peace so powerful that it defies our circumstances and provides inner rest so strong it overcomes the tumult and storms of life. That isn't to say that our problems aren't real or that they don't have consequences—but how we respond, how we walk through our storms, can be different. It can be a response of peace and rest as we partner with the Spirit day to day—moment to moment. A mysterious joy comes when we learn to rest in him even while our problems threaten to overwhelm us.

Jesus' promise in John 14:23 is that if we love him, he and the Father will come and make their home in us—right here within us—our spirit, our heart has become an inner temple where Jesus and the Father are ever present by the Holy Spirit dwelling in us—remarkable! Have you ever thought about the implications of that? The promises Jesus makes to us are right there, dwelling in our hearts, ready and at hand. We don't pray for his peace and have to wait for a response from some far off place. His peace is dwelling within us through Holy Spirit.

A little further, in verse 27, Jesus says *"Peace I leave with you; my peace I give you. I don't give to you as the world gives. Do not let your hearts be troubled and do not be afraid."* His promise to us is his very own peace shared with us. His peace is the kind that allows your heart not to be troubled or afraid when facing fearful troubles.

When I become overwhelmed by life, I often hear Jesus say to me, "Is \_\_\_\_ more powerful than my peace?" It isn't a mean question. He doesn't say it in a condescending way. He asks me in a gentle whisper. It brings my spirit back to a place of focus on him and I can't help but answer him, "No, Lord—\_\_\_\_ isn't greater than your peace." He is graciously teaching me and training me to stop, be still, and respond to this outer life from the place of his inner peace, resting in me by his Spirit.

In Isaiah 66, the beginning of the passage reads,
*Heaven is my throne,*
*and the earth is my footstool.*
*Where is the house you will build for me?*
*Where will my resting place be?*
*Has not my hand made all these things,*
*and so they came into being?"*
*declares the Lord.*

# REFLECTIONS FOR BURDEN BEARERS

*"These are the ones I look on with favor:*
*those who are humble and contrite in spirit,*
*and who tremble at my word.*

God declares that heaven is his throne and the earth is his footstool, the very picture of majesty and sovereignty. He made everything...everything belongs to him...he has everything...yet he has a question: who will build a house for him? Where will his resting place be? The people would have answered: the temple of course. The temple is your house and where your presence can rest. At the end of the second verse, God tells us the kind of person he holds in high regard: one who is humble and contrite in spirit—or someone who recognizes when they've done wrong, who has a genuine conscience. The rest of Isaiah 66 goes on to point out how sacrifices and rituals couched in religious observance don't mean anything to God when there is actually no spiritual substance behind them—the heart of humility and conscience is what God values and esteems.

In Matthew 11:29, we read, *"Take my yoke upon you and learn from me, for I am gentle and humble in heart, and you will find rest for your souls."*

Jesus is gentle and humble in heart; he is exactly the kind of person God is looking for in Isaiah 66. Jesus answers God's questions in Isaiah: Who will build a house for him? Jesus will build a house for him. What does that house look like? It is you...it is me...it is us...Jesus is the common link between us all...between us and churches and fellowships and communities meeting all over the world either in open or in secret. We are the house that Jesus has built for his Father, God. This was his intention, part of his mission. God's question was meant to show us something of the deep value he places on us. He wants his home to be with us. Otherwise, Jesus would not have made us his home. Recall what he said: *'if anyone loves me he will keep my word, and my Father will love him, and we will come to him and make our home with him'*—meaning he would make our spirits a dwelling place for his Spirit. The inner being of humanity is the place in all of God's vast and wondrous creation that he wants to live and make his home! He could make the most mind-blowing, amazing place ever and live there…yet he is so in love with you, that for him that most amazing place is within you.

Yet we are meant to be more than just a house for him, we are meant to be a place where his presence rests…where he abides…this isn't just a house: *it is home*. When you think of home, what do you think of? A home should be a place of rest, peace, safety, comfort, and joy. Home is where you go when you are done with working. It is the place you go to put your feet up and say, "Ahhhh, it's good to be home." That isn't always our experience, but it is what home is meant to be. In us, Jesus has been trying to create a home for God that is a place of abiding rest.

This is an amazing gift unfolding within us. Jesus is transforming us, creating in our hearts a place where God's presence may dwell. What kind of home will it be? Will it be a Jesus like home or something else? As we open our hearts to what Holy Spirit is doing within us, we are becoming a home that looks very much like Jesus.

Jesus gives us the promise of his peace. Through the work of Holy Spirit, we are becoming like Jesus. In this ongoing process, the home we make for God within us will be exactly like the home Jesus would make for God within himself. You become the house and home of God by allowing the presence of Holy Spirit to bring to life the character of Jesus within you. As we abide in him, we become like him. We are transformed into a home where God can say, 'Ahhhh, it's good to be home.'

Another amazing gift is that Jesus accomplishes this and offers it to us through an invitation. Who is invited? Listen:

are you weary and burdened (tired, bored out of your mind, hating life, exhausted, anxious, and stressed to the hilt?) Then come to me…I want you to come to me…I want to give you an answer for your weariness and burdens: **rest** (Matthew 11:28). God often doesn't deal with our struggles in the way we expect. God sees what we are lacking and invites us to find what we need in him. If you are worried and troubled, God out of his love and grace wants to give you peace and rest. He wants you to know and experience the reality that you can respond in a different way to the things that happen in your life, which are indeed stressful and troubling. This can be frustrating for us, because we want God to fix us like a divine mechanic. God won't opt for the quick fix because he is far more interested in transforming you into the likeness of Jesus so that you are never again in need of 'fixing' because you have been so deeply changed by his abiding presence. This is the hope of our transformation. Spiritual growth can be hard, but it is well worth it—and Jesus believes this more than anyone does. As we move deeper into the heart with Jesus, we will face some challenges, but they are always meant to bring us closer to God and to make us more like Jesus. The love of God is not the reward of transformation. Rather, the love of God is the energy moving us forward in transformation. The love of Jesus is a liberating presence, pouring grace into us where we are, leading us into true change. Our journey into becoming like Jesus begins in the atmosphere of his love, is constantly held in his love, and ultimately finished in his love. Understanding the nature and character of God's love—and how it differs from human love—is vital to the truly spiritual life we embrace as we choose to follow Jesus. Here, held in the embrace of his divine love, we find hope that even the most anxious of us can discover an inner peace that is far more powerful and profound than anything else we may explore. Our peace comes from a person who loves us so deeply that the Apostle John tells us that God *is* Love. Paul tells us that the peace of God transcends understanding—it will defy explanation at times as it rises up powerfully in the face of the storms that come our way (Philippians 4:7). This is the peace and rest of our heavenly Father. This is the promise of our Lord Jesus. This is the abiding presence of Holy Spirit.

Where will his home and resting place be? His home and resting place is in us. We are the place where God's presence abides. We are on a continuous journey of learning to be his home, but also we are learning, just as profoundly, how to make our home in him. As we grow in this exchange of abiding presence, he in us and us in him, we discover something at the very centre and core of God's nature: He is peaceful. He is at rest. He is filled with joy.

Are you weary? Are you burdened? I encourage you to answer Jesus' invitation. I encourage you to become a restful home for God's presence, which really benefits you the most, for it means you are allowing the rest and peace of Jesus to fill you…and that is a great place from which to live your life.

REFLECTIONS FOR BURDEN BEARERS
## Prayer

*Father, I thank you that you are the God of peace and rest, stillness and calm. Lord Jesus, I pray that you would draw near to my heart. I invite you to abide with me. I want to be a restful home for your presence, God. I ask that you would allow me to bring my burdens, my cares, my worries, and my stress to you. Jesus, give me your burden in exchange and give me your yoke. You promised that these would be easy and light, and I want to learn to walk with you in peace and rest. When life is overwhelming and troubles come my way, I pray that you would stand with me and allow me to know the peace of your Spirit. I want to be filled with your peace, which overcomes the storms of this world. When I am weak, Lord I know you are strong. When I am worried, I know you want to share your peace and confidence with me. Give me the grace to be able to stop and step back into your presence, so that I can see my circumstances through your eyes—your peaceful eyes, Jesus. Father, make me more than just a house…make me your home—Amen.*

**Scripture for Reflection:**
Isaiah 66
John 14
Philippians 4:7-9
Matthew 11:25-30
Psalm 131
Psalm 46

# Six
# The Light of the World

In our lives, we are often overwhelmed by the pain we sense and see all around us. At times, we may even weep over events that happen somewhere distant from us to which we aren't even connected in a personal way. The burden of Jesus comes upon our hearts as we witness the darkness in the world. At such times we weep with Jesus for the pain of others…we offer comfort to him in this way. Yet, always at such times of distress, there is a further invitation to pray. We are called to pray for the light of Christ to shine in the darkness, which neither understands Jesus nor can it overcome him. The light of Jesus lives within us as we open our hearts to him. From the windows of the home within us where he dwells, the warmth of his presence shines out.

In the Sermon on the Mount, Jesus says something remarkable: *You are the light of the world. A town built on a hill cannot be hidden. Neither do people light a lamp and put it under a bowl. Instead they put it on its stand, and it gives light to everyone in the house. In the same way, let your light shine before others, that they may see your good deeds and glorify your Father in heaven* (Matthew 5:14-16). Do you feel a little under qualified to be referred to as the light of the world? That is a high calling…and a daunting one. Yet, Jesus never puts a yoke on us he himself isn't willing to make possible. The good news is that you are the light of the world, not because of anything you do, but because he is the light of the world living in you.

In John 8:12 we read: *When Jesus spoke again to the people, he said, "I am the light of the world. Whoever follows me will never walk in darkness, but will have the light of life."*

Jesus is in the temple when he makes this declaration about who he is. The Feast of Tabernacles is going on at this time. Jesus speaks these words in what is known as the Treasury, where offerings are given. Here, close by, are four golden candelabra, with four golden bowls. Each one is filled from a pitcher of oil by a young man of priestly descent. The bowls of oil were lit on the first night of the Feast of Tabernacles. The light from these was so bright it could be seen beyond the temple throughout the city and on the surrounding hillsides. Jesus draws on what is around him to use as symbolic language for teaching his disciples and anyone listening. Imagine you are looking on and you hear him say, "I am the light of the world..."

If you were standing there, a curious onlooker attending the feast, what would you have heard in these words? Looking to the candelabra, you would have been reminded of a few things. First, when Moses and Israel were on their long and challenging journey from Egypt to the Promised Land, God's presence led them, as a pillar of cloud in the day and a pillar of fire at night. Light is God's presence with his people, guiding them and leading them out of slavery and into freedom.

Secondly, thinking about his words, you would have been reminded of Isaiah 49:6:

*And now the LORD says—*
  *he who formed me in the womb to be his servant*
*to bring Jacob back to him*
  *and gather Israel to himself,*

*for I am honored in the eyes of the* LORD
   *and my God has been my strength—*
*he says:*
*"It is too small a thing for you to be my servant*
   *to restore the tribes of Jacob*
   *and bring back those of Israel I have kept.*
*I will also make you a light for the Gentiles*
   *that my salvation may reach to the ends of the earth.*

God's light is salvation and it is a salvation meant to reach to the ends of the earth. It is meant to reach all people. It is not a salvation to be hoarded or selfishly hidden. After all, it is *light* and it shines no matter what anyone does. This salvation is always on the move dispelling and ending darkness.

More of Isaiah the prophet's words may have come to you as you heard Jesus speak:

*The people who walked in darkness*
*Have seen a great light;*
*Those who dwelt in the land of the shadow of death,*
*Upon them a light has shined.*

   *You have multiplied the nation*
*And increased its joy;*
*They rejoice before You*
*According to the joy of harvest,*
*As men rejoice when they divide the spoil.*
 *For You have broken the yoke of his burden*
*And the staff of his shoulder,*
*The rod of his oppressor,*
*As in the day of Midian.*
 *For every warrior's sandal from the noisy battle,*
*And garments rolled in blood,*
*Will be used for burning and fuel of fire.*

*For unto us a Child is born,*
*Unto us a Son is given;*
*And the government will be upon His shoulder.*
*And His name will be called*
*Wonderful, Counselor, Mighty God,*
*Everlasting Father, Prince of Peace.*
*Of the increase of His government and peace*
*There will be no end,*
*Upon the throne of David and over His kingdom,*
*To order it and establish it with judgment and justice*
*From that time forward, even forever.*
*The zeal of the Lord of hosts will perform this.*

Thinking on these words from Isaiah 9, you may have inwardly gasped, "Is he saying what I think he's saying?" The light ends the darkness and will bring about a new kingdom governed by genuine justice and righteousness. A kingdom in which people are free and live in peace, ruled by God, who is a wonderful counselor, a true Father in whom there is peace. Could this man standing here be this long awaited salvation in action?

I hope you can see that it is no small thing for Jesus to declare "I am the light of the world." He is saying he is the presence of God in the world and the salvation of God. He is the king who will rule the new kingdom of the age to come where there will be peace and freedom forever.

As if this isn't amazing enough he then promises: *Whoever follows me will never walk in darkness.*

When we choose to follow Jesus we follow him into a new place in the Spirit that we could never have entered without him. This is a place in the Spirit where darkness cannot follow…thus it becomes a place of freedom, a place of peace, a place of transformation and clarity. Light eliminates darkness. Imagine a dark room and what a single candle flame can do. Now imagine the glory of God shining from Jesus in the spiritual darkness of the world, into the human spirit and soul. It is a blazing light that puts summer sunshine to shame.

The darkness of sin gives way to the light of salvation and transformation. Once you were slaves to Sin, now you are sons and daughters of God in Jesus. The light has made a gate out of the darkness and is overcoming the effects of the Fall as we enter into a new kingdom. This is the kingdom of heaven and Jesus has brought you and I into a new family—the family of the Everlasting Father. Light reveals who God truly is and who we truly are to him. Do you know? This is the light Jesus brought to us: he came not only to save us, but to show us the truth of who God is...and it is good news! God is Love and he loves you. You are his child and you are loved...fully accepted, embraced, and cherished. Do you know that God cherishes you? You are the foremost thing on his mind. He hangs on every word you say and he loves to be with you and around you. Even when you are cranky, distressed, upset, depressed, under a cloud of darkness...he is the light surrounding you, filling you, and never giving up on you. His mission is to lead you out of spiritual darkness into his light of life where you are free and experience his peace and love. This is for you.

The darkness of death is shattered by the light of eternal life conquering it...death's dark sting is eliminated through Jesus. Death no longer holds its terrifying power over us, for it is not the end. This light of life we find when we follow Jesus is an eternal light and we will live with him now and forever. Do you ever think about that? How this day, right now, is part of a timeline that goes on forever? Yes we will pass through death along the way, but as the Lord once said to me, that is only a waypoint, a border crossing, along the way as we continue to follow him.

We will never walk in darkness as we follow Jesus. The depth of these words is even stronger in the original: it is unthinkable—completely impossible—for us to walk in darkness because Jesus is our light.

Then he tells us of the gift: *Whoever follows me will never walk in darkness, but will have the light of life.*
We are given the light of life. The presence of Jesus, the Holy Spirit...we have this light of life right here, living in us...his gift...his Spirit. Just as he would later promise his followers in John 14:15ff:

*If you love me, keep my commands. And I will ask the Father, and he will give you another advocate to help you and be with you forever— the Spirit of truth. The world cannot accept him, because it neither sees him nor knows him. But you know him, for he lives with you and will be in you. I will not leave you as orphans; I will come to you. Before long, the world will not see me anymore, but you will see me. Because I live, you also will live. On that day you will realize that I am in my Father, and you are in me, and I am in you. Whoever has my commands and keeps them is the one who loves me. The one who loves me will be loved by my Father, and I too will love them and show myself to them.*

This is the greatest gift, the light of life living in us. It is the guarantee of the promise of life and light, Jesus gave us. We have the light of the world waiting to shine out from within us so that we can invite others to join us as we follow Jesus...join us in becoming free from darkness and discovering the transformation of the life of Christ unfolding in our hearts.

We become the reflection of the light of life. When we follow Jesus and receive the light of life from him, we join him in becoming the light of the world. We are the mirrors through which he shines his light of life into the darkness of the world: we are the sign posts pointing to him. His light is seen in us and draws the people still living in darkness to him and into his kingdom of light. The light reveals the darkness of the world, but also opposes it. It is not enough to point out the darkness; we must always be declaring the light of Christ as the answer to that darkness and the victory over it. We need to tell of the salvation it offers to all people...all nations...to the ends of the earth.

We began with the words, *You are the light of the world*. These words can either be an overwhelming burden or a wondrous blessing. If we think they mean we must muster up strength in and of ourselves to do something, we will indeed be overwhelmed eventually. However, if we embrace the truth that Jesus Christ is the light of the world living in us, we find an invitation to a way of being in these words. To answer the call, we must lift our eyes to the one who is the light and surrender our hearts to him. As we create more room within ourselves for him, we will know him more and we will be filled with more of his light. We become the light of the world as we become like him because we love him and know him. We can't just be people who talk about the light, for in the end talk doesn't hold as much meaning as becoming like Christ does. A spiritual revolution within the heart is what Jesus offers us. This path is one of relationship. As we are transformed through our ongoing connection with Jesus we reflect the truth of his light and life. Perhaps the best way to think of it is to imagine ourselves actually becoming light. If you started glowing brightly in the middle of a darkened room filled with people, they wouldn't guess at what you were. Rather, they would know what you are. The only way to become light is to fix the eyes of your heart on the one who is light and allow his nature and character to shine through you. As we allow his light and life to flow through us we come to realize that his presence is with us always. We experience his guidance and his leading in our circumstances. We begin to see him at work in the midst of the darkness we thought might overwhelm us...his strength to save is greater than anything that would try to stop him. We encounter and then share the comfort, peace, and wisdom of his Spirit with others regardless of who they are, for this light is meant for all. The lamp is lit within our hearts and as we fall in love with Jesus, the light from the lamp cannot help but be seen.

## Prayer

*Father, I thank you for sending your Son to be the light of the world. Lord Jesus, I ask that you would fill me with your light and your life. I pray that the lamp of my heart would begin to shine more brightly and reflect who you are. Jesus, as I come to know you more, I pray that I would be transformed into someone through whom others begin to see you. Make me like you in my character and my actions. Help me to love others as you love them. Help me to see others the way you see them. I want to follow you and be so filled with Holy Spirit that darkness is pushed back because we are so connected. Help me to worry less about effort and to learn the deep joy of walking with you and knowing you, for out of our relationship your goodness and your power will flow through me to touch the lives of people in amazing ways. Lord, don't let me lose sight of who you are or how you are calling me to follow you as both your disciple and your friend. Thank you for filling my heart with your light...now help me to share all that it means with others in this world still struggling against darkness—Amen.*

**Scripture for Reflection:**
Ephesians 1:15-23
John 1
Isaiah 9
1 Peter 2
1 John 1:5-9

ERIC H JANZEN

Lord, fill our hearts
Lord, fill our vision with all
That you are
So that we know your glory
Lord, fill our hearts
We want to see you—only you
Jesus, Lord of kindness
Jesus, Lord of hope
Jesus, Lord of mercy
Jesus, Lord of love
Fill our hearts
With you—only you.

Soul of mine
Lift up your eyes
Look on the face
Of Christ
And wake, and wake, and wake up
Heart of mine
Open up your eyes
Look into the face
Of God
And wake, and wake, and wake up
He is here
He is our home
We are here
We are his home
So open up this
Heart and soul
And wake, and wake, and wake up

# Seven
# A Revealed Gift

Jesus does not wear a top hat, red coat, and black boots. He doesn't carry a whip with which to snap over our heads, driving us to leap through fiery hoops for his amusement. He is not a ringmaster in some unpleasant cosmic circus.

Are you relieved?

Too many of us have this image of Jesus floating around in our hearts. It is a lie we would be quick to discount if we heard someone describing him in this way. Yet, many of us carry around this misconception, allowing it to hinder our faith and our relationship with God.

Once, I had the opportunity to do some teaching from Matthew 11:25-30. I read the passage a number of times and felt…frustrated. It is a famous piece of scripture. Often, those can be the most difficult because they are too familiar. Jesus praises the Father for hiding the things of the kingdom from wise and learned folks and revealing the kingdom to little children instead. Not only that, but it pleased God to do so. "Why?" I wondered. He goes on to say, the Father commits all things to him and that no one knows the Father except for him. Jesus then says that those to whom he reveals God also know the Father. After this comes a wonderful invitation, but let's leave that for a moment.

## REFLECTIONS FOR BURDEN BEARERS

I decided I would ask Jesus about the first part of the passage. At first, all was quiet in my spirit. I wondered if I were perhaps too wise and learned to hear him speak to me on this (haha). A few moments later such an arrogant thought proved unfounded. Let me share with you what I felt him saying to me:

*"I have torn down the barriers of religion that kept people from the kingdom. The Gospel is given. It is revealed. I didn't want people to have to have scholarly degrees and learn several languages in order to receive my message. This is why I speak of revealing my Father. I came to show the world who God is, what he is truly like. I ended the need to adhere to a system of rules and protocols in order to feel there was a chance at knowing God and pleasing him. There is no peace in that kind of uncertainty and certainly no rest. I hid the kingdom from those who depend on unspiritual systems attempting to make the kingdom a matter of the mind instead of the heart. The kingdom is to be open to all, from the least to even the greatest, but it is given—not achieved."*

I sat back and considered what he was saying to me. He hides the kingdom from those who adhere to systems in order to connect to God. Throughout the Gospel story, we see Jesus at odds with such people. The Pharisees were always trying to trip Jesus up with the rules of religion, the system they believed was the only way to connect to God. However, Jesus teaches that the kingdom is revealed…it is open to all and given. You cannot achieve the things of the kingdom. Your connection to God comes out of a revelation of who he is and this is a revelation given through Jesus. This is good news! You should be feeling some relief after hearing him say this. The kingdom of heaven is committed to Jesus by the Father. In other words, Jesus is in charge of the kingdom and its unfolding presence in history. At the core of what has been committed to Jesus is the revelation of who God is. He didn't come and give us a new system. Rather, he came and gave us a full revelation of God. By the end of Jesus' ministry and life, he will have revealed to his followers that he is God and that to know what God is like, they need look no further than Jesus himself. Jesus has shown us the truth of God's nature and character.

In Matthew 11:28-30, Jesus gives a profound invitation in light of what he has just said to the people standing there listening to him. I imagine a small crowd of people looking a little stunned by his words. "Did he really just say that?" someone mutters (a phrase I imagine was said often when Jesus taught people). Another person nods, "Yeah, but will that really work? Revelation instead of system?" Alright, that last comment is probably what I would have said, but you get the idea. This is radical stuff. Jesus is turning things upside down and that would have been difficult for many people to hear and understand the first time around. Indeed, we are still having trouble catching on. Listen to his invitation:

*Come to me, all you who are weary and burdened, and I will give you rest. Take my yoke upon you and learn from me, for I am gentle and humble in heart, and you will find rest for your souls. For my yoke is easy and my burden is light.*

I have to tell you that sounds truly great to me. I am not a restful person. I get anxious a fair bit and, like many of us, I find it difficult to rest. If I do start to feel like I'm resting, an odd sense of guilt comes over me, as if to say, "If you aren't doing something, you must be doing something wrong." Jesus probably shakes his head at me from the throne room at these times and says something like, *"What do I have to do to get that guy to rest in me?"*

His invitation is a message of freedom from systems of rules that offer no substantial way to connect to God. Freedom from the exhausting sense of failure to live up to the 'rules', which are often nebulous and undefined in our day and age, behaving more like a heavy spiritual cloud weighing us down with guilt and shame. He frees us from striving to earn the things of the kingdom. Freedom from forcing a connection and relationship with God through a system telling us that if we were just a bit better, a bit more than what we are, we could maybe get there.

Jesus invites us to his Way. He gives us the kingdom through revelation. You can't attain it, because it doesn't need to be attained. Attempting to attain the kingdom outside of receiving the revelation of Jesus would be like trying to climb a mountain that simply isn't there. Jesus reveals the loving and amazing character of God to us in and through himself. He invites us to rest from the ways of the old system. Take a break from trying to earn God's acceptance and salvation. Rest from trying to earn his love, his grace, his mercy…you don't have to earn these things…they are a revealed gift.

Find the most comfortable seat in your home. Make a cup of coffee or tea…or whatever your favourite beverage may be, and sit down in that chair. Take a sip of your drink. Set it down. Take a deep, deep breath. Let it out and sink into the chair…rest. Now open your hands and lay them in your lap. Now get your courage up and get grateful. Turn the eyes of your heart onto Jesus and allow his presence to fill you, surround you. Welcome him and listen. He has so much to reveal about himself and the kingdom. Pause…rest…receive all that he wants to give to you. The presence of Jesus should always come with a light yoke and an easy burden. This is his promise…his invitation…his gift of freeing us from the weight of systems and leading us into the life of relationship with God.

I don't know about you, but that is a trade I gladly make.

ERIC H JANZEN
## Prayer

*Father, I thank you that you love us so much that you wanted your kingdom to be open to us all. Your intention is never to set up obstacles and barriers keeping people out of your kingdom. In fact, Father you have removed obstacles and barriers by your great grace and mercy. Lord Jesus, thank you for inviting me to enter your kingdom. I thank you for revealing your Father to us. Thank you for loving me and accepting me. I pray that you would heal my heart from believing that I have to earn your love by accomplishing tasks. I open the hands of my spirit to you and ask that you would fill me with a deeper revelation of who you are. Jesus begin to show me the deep things of the kingdom of heaven. Teach me to rest and to abide in you so that our relationship grows and matures in the foundation of your love for me. I am grateful for the gift you have given us through your revelation of the Father. Holy Spirit, I pray that you would help me to quiet my mind so that I can see and hear what you are saying and help me to become aware when I am striving to earn what you freely give. Help me to overcome my belief that there are barriers between us. I choose to believe that you have made a straight and open path for me, Jesus, so that I can know God through knowing you. Thank you for this freedom—Amen.*

**Scripture for Reflection:**
Matthew 11:25-30
Romans 8
John 3:1-21
John 6:43-71

# Eight
## Sin, Your Eyes, and Seeing God

As I sat in the back seat of a car, staring out the window at the landscape rushing by, I began to feel tired. My eyes grew heavy and I let them close. Then the gentle whisper of Jesus came to me and he said, *"Sin broke humanity's view of who God is and what He is like. You need me to show you my Father in powerful and heart changing ways."*

I sat there and stilled my mind. I wanted to just let his words sink in. Then I did what any modern person would do. I got out my phone, opened the 'notes' app, and wrote the words down. Then I set about doing what any ancient person knew to do…I began to ponder what he'd said.

Over the next few weeks I spent time thinking about it. I felt like there was a path to follow, so I looked for the beginning, which of course led me to The Beginning. In Genesis chapter 3 we have the account of the Fall of Man, which I sometimes think should be referred to more in terms of what was lost in the garden. We tend to emphasize the rebellion and fault we see—which certainly are obvious elements present in the account—but we also witness profound loss in this story. It is tempting to launch into a lengthy discussion of the Fall, but I will limit myself to a single point: humanity's loss of sight. At the Fall, Sin shattered human vision. It placed fractured spectacles upon our noses, through which we squint and blink, trying to see, but until those cracks are fixed we will be unable to see our way clearly. Sin broke our ability to see and know God as he truly is. We may be aware of him, but what we perceive of him is unclear… it is out of focus. But we are made to know God. We are made to worship him—indeed we are made for worship. So, despite our broken vision, we *will* seek something outside of ourselves and we *will* worship. In Romans 1:25, Paul writes, *"They exchanged the truth of God for a lie, and worshipped and served created things rather than the Creator—who is forever praised. Amen."* What is the truth of God? He is the one true God…the Creator. The lie exchanged for this truth about who God is? It is the sin of attributing the divine right to someone or something else and worshipping it as though it were God when it most certainly isn't. Yet, this is what happens when we cannot see and know God. If our ability to do so isn't healed then we will live a spiritual life that is either non-existent or one that is ultimately unfulfilled, frustrated, and broken. Honest spirituality wants to give worship where it is truly due, not just worship for worship's sake. Smash the idols and worship God is the rallying cry and essence of true religion, yet not out of pride, but out of an honest desire to connect with truth and with the reality of God. No shadow, no counterfeit will do. True religion seeks the truth.

So, back in Eden, Adam and Eve have eaten the mysterious fruit. Their eyes are opened, which is the moment the cracked glasses go over their vision, and Sin lays waste to creation like a cosmic hurricane followed by an earthquake of equal measure. The System is corrupted, changed terribly. When Adam and Eve looked around everything looked the same, but they knew it wasn't. Invisible splinters and cracks had filled reality like a shattering window. In Genesis 3:7-10 we see the result of this cataclysmic event when Adam and Eve encounter God for the first time after they're action and in verse ten we hear Adam express the core problem reflected in every human heart that would follow him. He's lost his ability to see and know God as he truly is…and now Adam *is afraid*. The majesty, authority, and the sheer awe inspiring power of God now intimidate Adam. He is terrified of his Creator. He no longer knows God's kindness and gentleness, he can't recognize the God who has come to walk with him in the garden and speak with him at other times. Everything has changed. Adam hides…"*I was afraid because I was naked; so I hid.*" He no longer feels safe in God's presence, he feels exposed—ashamed—so he hides. Adam and Eve's view of God—and consequently ours—has been so distorted by Sin that they cannot remain in the garden. They must leave for their own good lest they wither away in utter fear in the presence of God, unable to function. These truly are the deepest moments of loss in human history. The Golden Age crumbles into faded memory…though humanity spends the rest of history grasping for it, whether they agree on what it was or not, we all seem to know we lost the relationship with God we were meant to have and live only with a shadow of it. Yet there is an incredible message within this account of loss. God made us for worship…to live a life in relationship with him. God is not one to abandon his intentions and he cannot help but set out to deal with our sin-smashed glasses so that we will be able to see him and know him. Perhaps, this is the first thing all people need to know about God: he not only made us, but he loves us and wants to be invited into our lives even as he is inviting us into his own life. Yet, it can be extremely difficult for people to believe that the God of the universe even knows their name, let alone wants them to know him. When presented with this truth they find a way to hide from it. Much of our sinful lives are this attempt to hide from God, echoing the response of Adam and Eve from so long ago.

Jump ahead a few years now with me along the path of my pondering and we arrive at Moses. Now, if you think of any Old Testament character who knew God, you probably would think of Moses. Not only did he have a unique relationship with God, he seemed very confident in it. He was neither hesitant to make bold demands of God, nor shy about complaining to God about the fate he'd lain on poor Moses' shoulders. In Exodus 33 and 34 we see something curious. These chapters will be familiar to most avid Bible readers, but I hope to point out something that you may not have noticed before. Moses explains to God that he doesn't want to go forward with Israel on any kind of adventure towards a promised land unless God promises to come with them. Now, this isn't a request for God to simply accompany them. Moses wants God's dynamic, powerful, obvious presence to go with them. He wants to ensure that everyone they encounter knows that Israel is arriving with the most powerful God in the universe on their side. Moses knows that if God is seen and known for whom he is, no one will stand in the way of Israel and there will be nothing they can't accomplish. Moses is also wise enough to know that without God's presence with them, they have little chance going forward. Moses places extreme importance on God's presence being real and tangible in the life of Israel—his Glory is of the utmost importance. God is pleased with Moses' requests and agrees to do what he is asking, *"I will do the very thing you have asked because I am pleased with you and I know you by name."* Then in 33:18, Moses makes a bold request, *"Now, show me your Glory."*

## REFLECTIONS FOR BURDEN BEARERS

God agrees to show Moses his glory, but he sets out conditions before it can happen. Moses can only look upon God's glory and live if he is hidden in an opening in the rock, then covered by God's own hand, so that he won't look upon God's face. Sin is still exerting its power here. Moses will die if he sees God's face. We understand this in terms of God's holiness. His immense holiness was so potent that if Moses looked upon him he would die because of it. But, I wonder too if we can't recall Adam's plight here. Adam had seen God in the garden…walked with him and talked with him. When Sin fractured his ability to see and know God truly, then he could no longer look at him without fear and wanting to hide. If Moses, suffering with the same Sin shattered spiritual glasses had looked upon God's face *he would have been unable to see him for who he truly was*…he wouldn't have been able to hear God's words in 34:5 *"The LORD, THE LORD, the compassionate and gracious God, slow to anger, abounding in love and faithfulness, maintaining love to thousands and forgiving wickedness, rebellion and sin…"*. Instead of hearing God speak truth about himself, Moses would have struggled to survive looking upon the pure majesty and glory of God. God wants Moses to know him…what he is like, so he ensures that Moses is hidden in safety as the fullness of his presence comes to rest on him. In order to know God's glory, Moses couldn't look at or see God's face.

Let's journey down the path a little further and look in on Elijah. In 1Kings 19 we find the prophet in a cave. He's fled there after soundly defeating the false prophets of Baal at Mount Carmel in style. This was a showdown for the ages, and Elijah did more than just win it, he utterly demolished his opponents. So why has he fled to hide out in a cave? Elijah has trouble seeing things clearly. Jezebel, infuriated by his defeat of the false prophets, wants his head on a spike. When

God speaks to Elijah, the prophet is in despair, believing there is no one faithful to God in all the land except for him. God tells Elijah to get ready…he is about to come face to face with God's presence. In verses 11-13 a powerful wind blows, tearing up the mountains and shattering rocks…but God is not in the wind. An earthquake follows, but God is not in the earthquake. A fire comes, but God is not in the fire…these power filled manifestations of the elements would terrify any one present to witness them. Yet, Elijah waits. He knows something. I imagine a hush fell all around him as everything paused. Then comes a gentle whisper…*"When Elijah heard it, he pulled his cloak over his face and went out and stood at the mouth of the cave. Then a voice said to him, 'What are you doing here, Elijah?'"* Now God corrects his eyesight and makes things clearer for him. He is not the only faithful one in Israel, there are indeed seven thousand more. Elijah recognized the fullness of God's presence in the gentle whisper. What did he do? He knew to cover his face…he hides…he knows he can't look on the Glory and live. He won't hear the truth in God's words if he looks upon his face, for he will only be afraid of God and nothing else will be perceived or understood in the midst of his fear. Elijah's glasses are still cracked and distorted because of Sin—and I imagine he knew it.

Further down the path we must go. There must be an answer to the problem. If we are to know God the way he intends, then we need a way to overcome this broken and distorted lens through which we attempt to see and know him. Thankfully, God has made a way. As I pondered this vision issue, my journey brought me, as it always does, to Jesus. I often say that Jesus changes everything. In Jesus comes the upheaval of the spiritual landscape that has stood since Adam and Eve left the garden. He came to alter everything and to heal the ancient loss humanity experienced at the Fall. Recall that when he whispered to me, he told me the end I would come to after my pondering journey, *"You need me to show you my Father in powerful and heart changing ways."*

In John 14:5-9 we read something remarkable in light of what we have looked at along our path to this point. A change has come. A new era that would have filled any of the prophets with awe. Jesus is preparing his disciples for his departure. He's leaving them, but with a promise that he will return for them and that they know the way to where he is going. Thomas, not really sure what he means, needs clarification. They don't know where he is going so how can they know the way there? Jesus replies, *"I am the way and the truth and the life. No one comes to the Father except through me. If you really knew me, you would know my Father as well. From now on you do know him and have seen him."* As I read these words, I saw something in Jesus' statement I hadn't seen before. Why is it that no one can come to God except through Jesus? The answer lies in our distorted view of God because of Sin. It is only when we come to God through Jesus that we begin to see him as he truly is. Only Jesus can do something about our inability to see and know God. He is the revelation of who God is and what he is truly like in character. He is the expression of God's glory. Philip, perhaps so shocked by what Jesus has just said, asks for his own clarification in verse 8, *"Lord, show us the Father and that will be enough for us."* When Jesus answers him, I hear sorrow in his voice, *"Don't you know me, Philip, even after I have been among you such a long time? Anyone who has seen me has seen the Father. How can you say, 'Show us the Father'?"* This is a profound statement. Anyone present when he spoke these words would have known that an incredible revelation was being made along with an almost unbelievable change. They knew that no one could look on the face of God and live, and yet Jesus has just altered that reality. He is bringing humanity into a new relationship with God, or rather, restoring what was lost in the garden so long ago. A total change has come…you can see God and live. You can know him as he truly is, without distortion. In John 12:44 Jesus says, *"When a man believes in me, he does not believe in me only, but in the one who sent me. When he looks at me, he sees the one who sent me."* Who sent Jesus? God, the one true God, the Creator who walked with Adam and Eve in ancient days. Jesus is prophetically pointing to the new spiritual landscape that is about to be accomplished through his suffering.

So we come to the end of the path and we find ourselves at a familiar hill under overcast skies. Most journeys of reflection on the Christian life end up here. At the cross, Jesus takes action to do something about the cracked glasses humanity has been wearing over their eyes for so long. When Jesus overcame Sin and Death through his death and resurrection, he put an end to the fractured and distorted view of God that Sin had caused. I don't think that Jesus repairs the lenses in our spiritual glasses when we come to him. Instead, I've come to believe that he does something more profound than that: Jesus heals the very eyes of our heart so that we can see God for who he really is. Because of him we can look on the face of God and live. We come to life within, our spirits knowing in truth the love and compassion of God, the mercy and grace of his heart. When he draws near to us by his Spirit we are no longer afraid and driven to hide from him because we truly know that he cares for us. Because of Jesus we can know God. He has shown us the Father and revealed to us what was always meant from the beginning: our God is to be known. We are invited into his life and those who answer that invitation are never turned away.

One morning, some years ago, I wandered into the prayer tent we had at church where one could receive prayer during the worship time. I sat down and some friends began to pray for me. I found myself drawn into a place in my heart and began to see a vision there. I was sitting down in a chair and a figure approached me. I looked up and much to my astonishment found that I was looking at myself. I shared this with those who were praying for me. One of them suggested I try and ask a question of myself in the vision. "If you could prophecy something what would it be?" I didn't know what—if anything—would happen. Yet, no sooner were the words out of my mouth, than the vision version of me replied: "God is not angry with you."

The vision faded away as a well of emotion bubbled up and over, out of my soul and heart…and I cried…perhaps even wailed a little. I was a sobbing mess as many years of stored up guilt and shame simply erupted from my heart and left, lifted away by a truth spoken by Jesus through an odd vision. Since that day I have known without a doubt that God is not angry with me. That moment changed the way I knew him. It altered the way I prayed and approached him. I knew that I was a beloved and adopted son. Jesus had healed the eyes of my heart so that I could see and know God more deeply. We need Jesus to heal our eyes and reveal his Father to us in powerful and heart changing ways if we are to be truly spiritual people who want to know God as he truly is.

ERIC H JANZEN
# Prayer

*Father, I thank you for your love and compassion. I thank you for your commitment to healing the eyes of my heart and mind so that I can know you for who you truly are. Lord Jesus, I pray that you would show me your Father. Father, I pray that you would fill me with love for your Son. Holy Spirit, I pray that you would teach me and reveal to me the truth just as Jesus promised. I pray that you would take my picture and idea of who and what you are into your hands and heal what isn't right. I want to know you God. Like the disciples I confess that I haven't always understood who you are and the way to connect with you, but Lord I know that you are inviting me to a deeper revelation and relationship with you. Today, I open my heart more to you and invite you to touch my eyes and remove any remainder of the broken lenses my heart once wore. Thank you for walking with me in this journey of discovering who you are—Amen.*

**Scripture for Reflection:**
Genesis 1-3
Exodus 33-34
John 14
John 9:1-12

Unveil my heart so that I may see your face
Heal my ears, so that I can hear your voice of mercy
Make my path straight and true
Lead my spirit, Lord, ever and on to you

# Nine
# Faith in Crisis

In chapter 18 of John's Gospel we have the beginning of the end. Jesus has only just finished his prayer for both his disciples and all believers when Judas arrives with soldiers to arrest him. Jesus has completed his mission of teaching and revelation. He has completed his mission of sowing the powerful seeds of the gospel. Now he must face his suffering, taking on the final part of his mission as he acts to overcome Sin and Death. The dark horizon he's been journeying towards is upon him.

John shows us through his writing how Jesus confidently faces the end of his mission. His faith in the Father is uncompromising. He does not flinch before the Sanhedrin. He is bold in the face of Pilate's questions. He is going to the cross and nothing will sway him from embracing his suffering, for he is absolutely sure of, and committed to, his path. He will give himself for the redemption of the world. He will give himself in order to defeat the great enemies of his beloved creation: Sin and Death are going to be put under his feet. Not once do we see Jesus looking for a way out. His faith in his Father is awe inspiring.

Yet, in Matthew's Gospel we find a moment that took place earlier in a garden. In Matthew 26:36-46, we find Jesus in the Garden of Gethsemane. Here, Jesus wrestles with deep sorrow in the darkness of night. He faces his own suffering, sees it coming, all that it will entail, not only in this realm but in the spiritual realm as well, and he struggles with it. It is one of the most intimate moments we find in the gospel story, for we listen to Jesus speaking with his Father just as we, in our humanity, might have, *'O my Father, if it is possible, let this cup pass from me; nevertheless, not as I will, but as you will.'* He turns and finds even his best friends sleeping while his heart is overcome with the burden of what is about to take place. A second and third time he speaks with his Father... *'if this cup cannot pass away from me unless I drink it, your will be done.'* His friends sleep through his time of anguish. Jesus has walked through this lonely moment without them. If we read this passage of Scripture and allow our imaginations to take us there and hear Jesus voice as one filled with sorrow, we catch a glimpse of how difficult this was for him. Yet, he overcomes that place— *'Not my will, but your will be done'*—he responds to the Father. He puts his confidence in his Father and finds in his own faith the strength to follow the road forward. Later, when he comes to that dark horizon, his faith is strong—as we see throughout his response to the authorities who've taken him. In submission to the Father he finds the power to overcome—the hope that is described in Hebrews 12:2, *'For the joy set before him, Jesus endured the cross.'* Jesus carries the burden of humanity to the cross because of his relationship with his Father. In him, Jesus found the strength to move forward and accomplish the final part of what he came to do. This is why our own burdens find their destination in the hands of Jesus...he already carried them from Gethsemane to the Cross—and there he overcame them all. We don't find Jesus having a crisis of faith, for his prayer in the garden doesn't arise out of a lack of faith in the Father. His faith is steadfast, but his relationship with God the Father allows him to express the real emotions coursing through him. In Jesus, we find that we too can enter a garden at night and pray our own sorrowful prayers and ask our own questions...the real ones that are hard and may not have the outcome or answer we want. We learn to submit to the Father, trusting as Jesus did, that this path with him leads to joy even when we must endure a journey filled with sorrow and difficulty.

In the midst of Jesus' story we have another story; that of Peter. Recall John 13 where Jesus tells the disciples that he is going to a place they cannot follow him now, but will follow him to later. Peter, ever eager, asks where he is going and tells Jesus that he will follow him there even if he has to lay down his life to do so. Jesus challenges him *'Will you really lay down your life for me? I tell you the truth, before the rooster crows you will disown me three times!'* Later, as Jesus faces the political and spiritual powers arrayed against him, bent on ending his trouble making and seeking to quell his message, Peter must face his own dark horizon. He must face his weakness, his fear, his fragile faith. I find this story compelling. I love the humanity in it...the honest reflection of the heart. Peter has a crisis of faith. At the point of each denial we can guess that Peter is in an intense emotional, mental, and spiritual spiral.

What's happened? How can his Master have been betrayed and arrested? Why would he simply give himself over to the authorities? Clearly, Jesus has the power, real power to resist his enemies. They fell over when they came to arrest him, presumably knocked down by the mere power of Jesus' Godly presence. A thousand questions would have been swirling around in Peter's mind and heart, boiling down to one, *"How can this be happening?"* Doubts assailed him. He walked with Jesus for years…witnessed the kingdom of God acting powerfully through Jesus' touch, words, and prayers. *How can this be?* He denied Jesus a third time and the rooster crowed. How Peter's heart must have stilled in that moment, stricken to the core by the prophetic power of the sound of the rooster. I imagine him standing as still as a statue, the sound echoing through his soul. *I've done as he said I would. I've failed him utterly.* Peter's heart breaks as he faces the crisis of faith that has befallen him.

Is this your story? It's certainly part of my story. I've lost myself in anxiety and depression. I've lamented in the night, asking God why he is so distant. Are you there? Are you listening? I've doubted my faith and faced deep inner crises of faith. I've been overwhelmed by the world and its corruption, the seemingly unstoppable tidal wave of evil that spreads across every nation in the world in one way or another. I've sat in stunned silence asking, 'If you are alive, Jesus, how can this be?' I think moments of crisis in our faith are part of our journey with Jesus. Like Jesus and Peter, we all face these moments of deep pain and sorrow where our faith takes a beating. Jesus finds hope in his Father and overcomes the crisis before it can break him.

Peter is broken. The rooster has crowed and he shuffles off into the night to weep in sorrow for his failure. How long was it before he recalled the entirety of Jesus words to him in John 13? There was a seed of hope offered to Peter: '*Where I am going you cannot follow now, but you will follow later.*' Once when I was reading, this verse I felt Holy Spirit say, '*Peter would later recall these words and they gave him hope. They helped to heal his broken heart. He knew that though he'd failed on that night, his faith crumbling away, he would overcome that failure and follow Jesus exactly in the way his heart truly desired.*' Even when our faith is weak or failing, Jesus imparts hope to those who follow him.

I remember getting ready for work years ago. It was a job I didn't enjoy at all. I looked in the mirror with a heavy heart, and the Lord spoke to me, *"Today, I am releasing you from this job."* I shook my head to clear my thoughts. That couldn't be the Lord could it? Sure enough, I arrived at work and my manager called me into the office. I lost my job. I felt terrible, but I was also filled with a little awe. Less than an hour before, Jesus had let me know this was going to happen and I knew that he was with me in the midst of it. He wasn't panicked; he already knew what was coming and was ready to guide me into the next season of life. It wasn't easy. In fact, the next few years were very difficult, yet filled with his companionship, his action, and his love. My faith was stretched, but I always had a seed of hope to hold onto because he'd spoken to me before anything happened. As I've grown older and reflected on my life a little more, I've begun to see more than one such seed of hope. I'm beginning to marvel at how Jesus has been walking with me and speaking to me in so many different ways, inviting me to deeper faith and always sharing his hope with me in the darkness and in troublesome times.

This is the hope Jesus is holding out for us today, for his mercies are new every morning. He calls us to follow him. He calls us daily to himself when we wake and when we lay our heads down to sleep. By his grace, his mercy, his power, and his generous love, we can know that despite a crisis of faith, we can follow him, embracing his will for our lives. I think in Gethsemane, Jesus won a strength of faith not only for himself, but one he gives to us now by his Spirit. By that infilling of faith, we too can embrace the mission of Jesus, the message of his gospel, with confidence and strength. When we ask for faith, Jesus gives it willingly…happily. Let us put our hope in him and follow him as we truly desire to in our hearts, not allowing past or present crises of our faith to stall us or stop us. We are not only called to overcome…but we are empowered *to* overcome by the gift of God's Spirit within us through whom a deep faith flows to us and causes our own to grow.

## Prayer

*Father, I thank you for listening. I thank you that you are a God who can hear the prayer of pain and sorrow, angst and even anger. Lord Jesus, I'm grateful that you showed us how God never turns away from us even when we need to pour out the chaos arising within our hearts. Holy Spirit, I pray that you would fill my heart with the faith of Jesus...I believe, help me in my unbelief. God, you know that there are times when I have questions, doubts, and disappointments. I pray that you would help me to enter into your presence when I am walking through these things. I am amazed that you are willing to work through all of them with me. It is one more aspect of who you are that shows me how much you love us. When the burdens of this world and my life are overwhelming, Lord I invite you to draw near to me. I thank you that your hands are open and ready to receive what weighs my heart down. Thank you for the hope you so freely share with me. Help me to connect with your faith, hope and love—Amen.*

**Scripture for Reflection:**
Matthew 26:36-46
John 18:12-27; John 21:15-19 Read these two passages together.
Psalm 34
2 Corinthians 1:1-11
Isaiah 41:1-20

# Ten
# The Dark Night of the *What!?*

One day as summer was approaching a number of years ago, I made a mistake. I don't mean the kind of mistake where you've done something wrong and now you've got to face a consequence, because it wasn't like that. No, this is one of those mistakes any seriously spiritual person, honestly seeking after God, will eventually make—and we make it because we are either ignorant or naïve. I think I was a little bit of both, with a dash of the old Janzen arrogance thrown in for good measure. Looking back now, I realize that Jesus wanted me to make the mistake, and thus did little to warn me…sigh…such is love.

The tale begins in a church—as such things ought to—where I sat enjoying the teaching of one of my favourite prophetic teachers. It was Jon Paul Jackson for those who must know, though what he said at the time has little to do with my story. I was minding my own business, paying attention, when Holy Spirit rudely interrupted. He brought to mind a frustration that had been growing in me for quite a while and seemed to pour a little extra energy into it. I sat there squirming in my seat trying to ignore him, but as you can imagine that only made things worse. He began to speak.

I'll reproduce the conversation below…the Holy Spirit will be in Italics:

*"What is that frustration you've been feeling in your spirit?"*

"You know what it is, Lord."

*"Are you going to talk to me about it?"*

"Sure. I've been feeling confused and getting angry at all the different voices out there telling me what Jesus is like, and who he is, and what he cares about, when it seems like nobody can agree on the answers to those questions. I want everyone to just shut up and quit telling me what to believe."

*Silence, but not that silence which is empty…it was that silence he uses to draw you into the next moment, the moment where he lets you take a step that you have to freely take, because He will never coerce us.*

"You know what I want, Lord? I want you to tell me about who you are and what you're like. I want to really know you. So…I invite you to come and sit with me at a table with two chairs, somewhere private. All I want is you, Lord. I just want to hear from you what you say about yourself."

*"Very well …."*

"Amen?"

And that was it. I'd made the mistake. I'd crossed a threshold I couldn't turn away from and I felt it, though I couldn't understand why I was feeling a mixture of excitement and unease. I think the excitement was God's and the unease was coming from my own heart. Some part of me realized I'd just taken my first steps onto the road of the dark night of the soul, what some call the desert, and my soul was shaken, trembling with trepidation. Yet, as I mentioned above, I was largely ignorant of the path I'd begun. If I had any inkling, I was naïve enough to think it wouldn't be that bad—and the Good Lord knows my ego would just give a high-five and a cheer to my naïveté with some kind of bold, yet stupid comment like "Bah, we can handle it!" Of course, such bravado is one of the first illusions stripped away in the dark night along with many others. Like the passing of a season, it would take some time before I realized what had happened—and by then I was so far down the road there was no way but forward. My mistake had become the journey God intended all along—this was a plan and not a mistake at all.

In the early days, when the dark night was perhaps still the dark evening, I faithfully prayed the prayer I'd committed to. My faith in God had reached a vital frontier at this time. I'd finally grown out of a complacent season, a time where I was content to kind of coast along. Something had sparked a passion in my heart and I was happy to find it there. Out of my frustration over wanting to know God on his own terms, I had grown thirsty once more, hungry for Him. I thought this was an excellent sign of spiritual maturity and I have to admit I was expecting a far quicker answer to the thirst and hunger than was to come. Self-righteous arrogance is another illusion we lose in the dark night along with all of its tendencies towards fast food delivery spirituality—amen good riddance.

For the next two months, I prayed daily and nightly, asking Jesus to simply meet with me at a table with two chairs in a private place. There were a few brief moments of conversation between us, and they were good as it is always good when Jesus speaks with us, but there was nothing earth shattering about those exchanges—or so I thought. Mainly, Jesus would tell me in some way that he loved me. The simplest of truths, yet always the most difficult for us to truly hear, and I was no exception.

Then on a mid-summer night I fell asleep and awoke in a vision, which I recorded in my journal:

\*

## REFLECTIONS FOR BURDEN BEARERS

*I was dreaming that I was hiking up a mountain. It was very dry, arid as I imagine a desert would be. I was on a dirt road, sunny day etc.... I came to a small town on the mountain and there were people milling about. I became aware I was dreaming when I saw my brother walking with his twin brother. This is impossible since he doesn't have a twin brother!*

*"I am dreaming and in a vision," I said. The twins approached me and I said to them, "I know I'm dreaming and in a vision, so tell me what you represent."*

*One of the twins transformed immediately into a gift box floating in mid-air before me and I reached out to take the gift box. It transformed into a handful of coins in my hand. "I get it," I said. "Change—you represent change."*

*Then the town and everyone disappeared. I continued to be quite aware and began walking further up the mountain.*

*I called out, "Jesus, I know you don't have to, but can you show me how much you love me?"*

*Out of the corner of my eye I immediately saw a very bright light flash and when I turned to look at it I saw him. I saw Jesus standing there clear as day. He was smiling and held his arms out to me. I ran to him and embraced him and began to cry. It was incredible, for I could feel him physically—just as real as though I were awake. I held onto his arms and could feel them in my hands.*

*"Thank you for everything you've done for me," I said. "Thank you for saving me."*

*I looked into his face and he was smiling and crying as well.*

*"Thank you for saving me," I said again.*

*"I proved you wrong," he replied.*

*"Thank you for saving me," I said once more.*

*"I proved you wrong," he replied again.*

*Then I asked him what this place was and he said "Miranda."*

*I looked around and saw that we were standing at the top of the mountain. There were objects resting here, but what really grabbed my attention was this: there was a small cave with a table and two chairs in it.*

*Then I woke up.*

*Aside from this being one of the most incredible experiences I've ever had, seeing Jesus face to face like that (an encounter I've prayed for, for such a long time) I am confused by what he said. I don't know what to make of his response "I proved you wrong."*

*"Miranda" is a name that means 'worthy of admiration'.*

\*

It's funny to look back at journal entries sometimes. I laugh when I read this one and get to the line 'Then I woke up.' It was more like bolting straight up, breathing like I'd been swimming underwater, and blinking my eyes rapidly trying to orient myself. There is a lot that could be said about the experience of this kind of vision, but such considerations aren't really pertinent to the story, except to stress that I was fully aware of what was going on in the vision and I can't express in words how real it all was, you'll just have to try and imagine it. The vision left me shaken. I walked about in a daze the whole next day; it was difficult to concentrate on regular life. I kept revisiting the scenes of the vision, pondering what it might mean. And then I did something I rarely do: I drafted an email and sent out the vision to several trusted friends. I needed help. *I needed help.* Now, of course, needing help is nothing extraordinary, but my asking for help is. I don't like to do it. I like to figure things out on my own and do things on my own. But God had blinded my eyes and before I really got the point, I had hit 'send.' Self-sufficiency is another bad habit that gets torn down as you walk in the dark night. Heads up: that's a tough one.

Let's break down the vision a bit.

There was some of the vision that was straightforward. In the first part my brother turns into a gift box that turns into change: okay, Lord you are about to cause some kind of change in my life and it is a gift. Then there is the location: a mountain top...okay, Lord you like to use mountaintops for significant spiritual encounters with your people, which this vision certainly was for me. But note: the mountain is a desert mountain and I know enough to equate that with the dark night of the soul...now I'm a little nervous about the change that he is 'gifting' me. Then we hit the portion I don't get at all at first: *I proved you wrong.* What does he mean by that? Why did he say it more than once? Second: why is the mountaintop called 'Miranda'? But one of the most amazing things about the vision was seeing the table and two chairs in the cave. This was the place that I'd been praying for! The place I had been inviting him to meet me in. Now, if I could just understand what He was saying there it would really be incredible.

Then a friend replied to my email. He wrote: "Miranda is probably what he proved you wrong about. I.e., part of you does not believe you are worthy of admiration. That sense is what sometimes puts you in the dry climb and is what needs to change. Saving you and visiting you in your dream both prove you wrong. This special visit says something about how special you are to him."

I read his response to my email several times and could feel God's presence surrounding me, as though to say *"Pay attention, Eric."* My friend had seen what I couldn't on my own. With his help, I was able to see how Jesus had chosen to respond to my request and at the heart of what he wanted to tell me was that he loves me. He loves me in the way that I only dare wish for...that he would meet with me face to face. Another friend pointed out to me in another email response that to 'mirandize' someone is to tell them what their rights are, as police do when they arrest someone. Jesus was showing me that it was my right to meet with him, to know who he is, and what he's really like.

As with all great heights of spiritual experience, I had to descend from the mountain. Jesus had planted the seed, prophetically showing me the end of a journey I hadn't yet completed. The dark evening was ending and the dark night was about to fall.

## 2

This is not the kind of spiritual journey you wish on anyone. Nor is it the kind of story that will inspire people to seek a deeper relationship with God. No, if they see the dark night for what it is really like, they may wisely dig a hole where they are, set up a nice tent, and remain there. Many do, I imagine. However, I must confess some of my negative commentary is not to be taken to heart…too much. The point is this: the dark night of the soul, or the desert season, isn't something to be taken lightly. It is hard. I can recall many conversations in which someone has commented, 'I've been in the desert for three weeks…finally coming out of it.' No. That wasn't the desert. The dark night lasts much longer than three weeks or three months. It is a long haul that takes us into a deep valley where darkness lingers and every step presents a challenge. This is the valley of honesty, the valley of relentless pressure pushing in on the soul. As you descend into this valley, your heart skips a beat, your breath catches in your throat, and you have to dig into your courage to take the steps forward. As I did this, I kept the treasure of my vision of Jesus close to my heart. It was a prophetic promise for me to hold on to. It gave me an anchor of truth to call upon when the valley sought to claim me. Jesus loves me. I am worthy of his love…even his admiration. And it is my right to know him and be loved by him.

## REFLECTIONS FOR BURDEN BEARERS

As I have journeyed through the dark night I have struggled in ways I never thought I'd have to. I've learned what Paul meant when he wrote of groaning as prayer in Romans 8. That groaning of spirit was at times the only expression left when spiritual frustration became so overwhelming that I had no more words to express how stuck I felt. This is one of the first recognizable characteristics of the dark night, or it was for me. You feel like your strength and energy are being sapped, your feet mired in unmovable ground. Straining every muscle to try and move forward becomes exhausting and maddening. In those moments I've prayed, "Why? Why are you keeping me here? Stuck like a statue?"

It turns out that this is an excellent question to ask in the dark night. *Why?* is the point isn't it? Jesus didn't lead me into the dark night to grant me the next warm and fuzzy spiritual experience. He'd led me there to find him. I had willingly entered because I wanted to know God on his terms. The dark night is about removing the obstacles to that goal...but the mystery is how much we learn about God as we endure that dark night. I've asked the question "why?" many times during my desert sojourn. Each time I was finally able to face the answer, I found myself having to deal with a serious heart issue, and some of them were quite surprising to me. This was the light of Jesus shining on the most uncomfortable recesses of my heart and he was showing me things I wasn't even aware of. This is another mark of the dark night. We begin to experience emotions and attitudes and sin in our lives that take us by surprise. I won't go into detail about everything...as that would be too humiliating. I will speak of a few though.

The first alarming area that Jesus relentlessly delved into was my anger. Anger? Those who know me might find that surprising. I know I did. The dark night of my soul revealed a deep well of not only anger in my heart, but what I would even call—at times—rage. I was angry, but I wasn't sure why. It was there, bubbling like a pool of lava beneath the earth…smoldering away and only emerging in brief flashes before being hidden away again. Well, God had a plan to unleash that well of anger, pushing buttons to elicit some temper tantrums that were, apparently, long overdue. I recall leaving an evening session at a conference I was attending. The teaching had been good—the worship time even better. I was feeling pretty good. I got on the freeway, heading for my favourite coffee shop to visit with some friends. Traffic grew thick…my heart began to sink…red tail lights could be seen ahead at a standstill for as far as the eye could see. As I slowed down and joined the stalled traffic, I could feel my well of anger stirring.

"Keep calm," I told myself. "It's not that big of a deal."

However, forty-five minutes later, no cars had moved at all. I was trying so hard to be reasonable, not to let my frustration boil over, but abruptly I felt my carefully measured self-control crumbling. I was seething. I was truly angry. My analytical brain whispered from some distant place that I was overreacting, but the rest of me didn't care. I lost it. I won't share the colorful language that escaped my lips, but I vented like you wouldn't believe. The lava flowed up and out, boiling over and filled my car with its raw heat. By the time I calmed down, I felt like I'd been running…and I was ashamed. Then, for the first time in a while, God spoke to me.

*"That was me."*

"What?" I said.

*"That was me. I prodded at your heart to release all that anger."*

"Why? Why would you do such a thing?" (You ought to imagine a flabbergasted and whiny tone in those words.)

*"Your anger has been building for most of your life. You have stowed away years of hurt and it became a well of anger in your soul. Left unchecked, your anger would eventually lead to some very serious issues*

*in both your spiritual life and your most important relationships. That is not what I want for you. I want your anger so that I can fill that place in your heart with my Presence."*

This made me pause. Most of my life? What was he talking about? As I sat there looking out my window at the red brake lights shimmering in the night, they began to blur. My anger spent, now it was time for the pain I'd been harboring to emerge. I began to cry…and I cried for a long time. There are no words for this moment. As I look back now, I can see Jesus sitting in the car with me, just being with me, his hand on my shoulder. He wasn't there to help me stop crying, he was there to make sure those tears flowed and kept flowing…I realize now he was healing many hurts all at once. When that moment finally subsided, I blew my nose and leaned back. I felt like I'd been running again, but this time it felt like I'd passed a finish line. Then he spoke once more: *"I have a question for you. Why do you feel ashamed if you express your anger when someone hurts you?"*

"I don't know," I replied.

And that was it. He'd given me something very important to think about and it took me a long time to figure it out. At the root of my particular issue was (and is) a strong dislike for conflict. Most of you would probably say you feel the same way. After all, conflict is unpleasant. My problem was that I so disliked and feared conflict, I would simply refuse to engage in it. If someone hurt me, I would work very hard to bury that hurt and forget about it. I wasn't one to confront someone and share with them how they hurt me, let alone attempt to reconcile that hurt. Oh what an ugly realization this has been. It is still a challenge for me. But, I have changed the ways in which I respond to being hurt. In the Gospel I have found an important key to ensuring that well of anger doesn't reoccur within my heart. I have discovered that genuine mercy and forgiveness are powerful weapons against bitterness and anger. I've learned to walk through hurts with Jesus before they can be bottled and stored away to become a future problem. Not always an easy process, but after what Jesus took me through that night, I've learned to remain committed to his Way of dealing with hurt and not my old way.

One more example of Jesus' relentless surgery on my soul is probably needed. This one is an area that I'm sure many can identify with: Anxiety. I can't say for sure, but I'm fairly certain I was born anxious. I have always been a shy, introverted person. I used to struggle with this, but as an adult one of my greatest victories was accepting that this was part of how God created me. Perhaps that's another story though. However, my anxiety problems often arise from my shy nature. There may be some that read this and recall awkward one on one conversations they've had with me and now can know the reason why. If I don't know someone well, it is difficult for me to speak with them, though I always do my best. My anxiety goes well beyond a social anxiety though. Throughout my marriage, my poor wife has often had the following conversation with me:

"What's wrong?" she asks, for she is astute and knows when something isn't right with me.

"I'm anxious. I'm worried," I reply.

"About what?"

"I don't know," I respond.

That's tough for her. How do you help someone who can't give you a reason for what they are feeling? Now, I've learned over the years that as a burden bearer some of my anxiety level is often not even my own, but a burden I have been carrying on behalf of others who are worried and anxious about things in their own lives. But not all of my anxiety could be explained by this. Simply put, I find it difficult to be at peace in my heart. In fact, Jesus himself has had to endure the very same conversation with me as my wife has. He, though, is able to take things a little deeper. As I have travelled along the valley road through the dark night of the soul, Jesus has returned to this area of my spirit again and again. He has been challenging my anxiety issue head on and with good reason. Repeatedly, in the Gospels, Jesus makes some very strong promises about peace and freedom from worry and being anxious. It clearly is not his desire for me to live life hunched over, feeling stressed out about things I can't even name, let alone the real concerns of daily life. No, he wants me to experience the peace of his Presence in real or imagined situations that cause me anxiety. He is the answer for my worrying soul. In the midst of the dark night this was very hard for me. Already feeling stuck and spiritually dry, trying to overcome anxiety seemed like an impossible feat. But this was a journey with different stops along the way and at each, though I couldn't 'feel' the healing, Jesus was working within my heart to make a place for his peace to rest…to abide.

One night, I finally saw evidence of this. My pattern—for years—has been to go to bed, lay my head down on the pillow, and do two things. First, I review my day. I think about all the things that happened, the things I may have said or done. What was good about my day? What was bad? What could I have done differently and what did I do well? And what is there to be concerned about? What will tomorrow bring? And the next day? Oh and next week I will have to…on and on it can go. You can see what happens. I quickly descend in a spiral looking for the things I need to put on my worry list. Needless to say, this is not a good habit, but it is a long standing one. The second thing I do is pray. I talk God's ear off in the early morning hours. I don't sleep well…never have, so I spend that time talking to God. On this night I began my ritual and had to pause. Something was wrong…well different might be a better word. I realized that I had gone the entire day without feeling anxious. I hadn't worried about anything. It was so striking that I lay there blinking to make sure I was awake. There was an unfamiliar lightness in my spirit and now that I was in bed in the silence of the night, I recognized it. *Peace.* My heart was peaceful. I remember thinking to myself, "So this is what that feels like."

I then began my nightly prayer time.

"Lord, did you know that I went a whole entire day without feeling anxious?"

*"Yes."*

"I don't how that could have happened."

*"I've been working deep within your heart for a long time now. I want you to know my peace. Today there was little for you to worry about, but my peace is meant to rise up in you even on the days when there are very real worries that arise in your life. When your spirit becomes anxious you have forgotten my promise that I will never leave you nor forsake you. I stand at your side in all things. I am teaching your spirit to embrace my peace instead of becoming anxious. I want you to come to a place in your heart where leaning on my peace becomes your first response in all things, instead of reacting to them with anxiety."*

I took a moment to take these words in and something dawned on me. This progress had taken a long time. "This is a major issue isn't it?" I stated more than asked.

*"Oh yes, Eric. Your anxiety was rooted so deeply in your heart that I have to take time and gently heal it. Today you have experienced the fruit of what I have been doing…and there is more to come."*

More to come. It may be difficult for some to understand just how amazed I was at that time. It was the first time I could remember in my life that I had been inwardly peaceful for an entire day. The mystery in all of this is that I hadn't *done* anything. In fact in this area, I was my own worst enemy. I can't sit here and write out some detailed system for how to be a little more spiritual or give advice on how to overcome anxiety. This was God's work. This was the light shining in the darkness of the long night. This was God's mercy at work in my heart because he loves me.

It was after this prayer time with Jesus that something shifted in my life. A light appeared in the distance. I peered ahead and wondered, "Could that be the end of this valley? Is my time in the dark night of the soul finally nearing its end?"

Not quite. Something else was about to happen that has had a profound effect on me to this day. And in the end, it was a bit of a no-brainer.

## 3

In the midst of the dark night of the soul I clung to scripture like a man thrown overboard into the sea might cling to a piece of driftwood. During this time I became anchored—or stuck—in Paul's letter to the Romans at a familiar point: Chapters 7 and 8. Chapter 7 is not for the faint of heart. Here Paul launches into a complex and sometimes confusing discussion of the law, sin, death, and the twists and turns of the human heart in relation to them all. I won't pretend to try and discuss this as well as real scholars might, but I have to talk about it in light of the harrowing tale I'm relating here.

One of the surest signs that we are in the dark night of the soul is our confrontation with Sin. It isn't that sin becomes worse in your life. What becomes worse is your awareness of your sin. It becomes overwhelming as you begin to see it more clearly, perceiving it more acutely. As this happens your own desire to overcome Sin grows sharply, but the spiritual strength to do so simply isn't there. In the dark night of the soul, weakness marks you as surely as a tattoo marks skin. In this place of awareness and weakness occurs something only Jesus can do. He begins to transform you, because the truth is this: Jesus has overcome Sin; he has overcome the spiritual rot and death that Sin causes. It is only as we turn to him that we find strength outside of our weakened selves that can help us in the face of this brutal power named Sin.

Yet, we must be willing to do this one thing. We must turn to him. We can choose not to and proceed to bash our fists into the face of an enemy we can't defeat alone. In the end this is nothing but an exhausting battle that leaves us spent, frustrated, and despairing. In the dark night of the soul we become aware of our fallen humanity. The wise become humbled by their shortcomings and *embrace their need for mercy*. Here in this place we learn one of the most important things about being Christians: just as we receive mercy we become merciful. We don't just learn about mercy, we become those who truly understand what it is like to receive it, and out of that humbling experience, we become able to show and give it to others. In the dark night we discover Christ's generosity towards us, an ever present outstretched hand of mercy and forgiveness that refuses to abandon us even when we aren't even sure if he is there. This struggle with Sin in the dark night comes at what seems like the worst possible time. In the dark night we are already at our most vulnerable, feeling weak, frustrated, stuck, doubtful, empty, and often alone. What a perfect time to learn just how much we need Jesus.

Of course, it is easier to look back on a struggle and reflect on it than it is to reflect on the struggle when you are angrily walking through it. I was in a very deep hole as I faced Sin. I felt at times that I was dying inside. What made it all the harder was that I couldn't talk about it with anybody. I didn't know how to articulate what I was going through. I found comfort in the Jesus Prayer, which gave me words to lift to God when I had no inspiration of my own. The Jesus Prayer remains central to my prayer life to this day, for it became an anchor for my heart and thus a treasure as well. Daily, I began turning to the mercy of Jesus. I read Romans 7 and 8 almost every day, because the second half of chapter 7 seemed to put words to what I was feeling and going through and chapter 8 was where I wanted to go. Here are some highlights.

In Romans 7:13 Paul answers a question about whether the law itself, being good, could have caused such a negative outcome as death. Listen to his words instead of me:

*"Did that which is good, then, become death to me? By no means! But in order that sin might be recognized as sin, it produced death in me through what was good, so that through the commandment sin might become utterly sinful."*

I began to see what Paul was trying to say when I was feeling like sin was killing me on the inside. It truly does choke out the life within our spirits. I was recognizing sin in a far more profound way than I ever had before. So, the law is good in that in its light, sin becomes fully exposed for the incredibly destructive power it is. Paul goes on in that chapter to describe a very familiar pattern of failing to do what in our hearts we want to do and doing the very thing we do not want to do. I like these verses because they don't take the fight with Sin lightly. This is an honest description of what the inward life looks like when the battle is happening. I found that Sin gives rise to an inner conflict between the true desire in my heart to be like Jesus and to satisfy sinful desires—whatever those may be. Sometimes I felt like I was two people, though I well knew I wasn't. I had come to understand that sin was more than a wrong act or something that kept me separate from God. Sin was a power...like a cloud of gas surrounding me, seeking to destroy me. I often echoed Paul's cry at the end of chapter 7 in verse 24, *"What a wretched man I am! Who will rescue from this body of death?"*

You can't stop there. I camped in that spot for too long, in my own opinion. I looked across a chasm at Romans 8, wondering how to get over there. A question began to occupy my thoughts: What is the bridge from the struggle described in Romans 7 and the life and freedom described in Romans

8? I began to slip this question into conversations when the opportunity arose. I was looking for something to spark a real answer. I ignored the platitudes and the self-righteous responses. One evening as I sat having coffee with a close friend, I asked him what he thought. It was a good conversation, but the kernel my spirit was seeking wasn't there. Then, a couple of weeks later I saw him again and he told me that he had been considering my question and had asked a few others what they thought. One friend of his, an older (and wiser) woman had told him that the answer was right there in the very next verse.

"Really?" I said

"Yes," he replied. "She said the bridge is in gratitude."

I hummed. I hawed. "Seems too simple," I said.

He grinned at me. "I think she's right."

"I'll let you know," I told him. Though I was skeptical, I had most certainly felt a spark in my heart at the word 'gratitude'. There was something very important here.

Romans 7:25 responds to the question in verse 24 with: *"Thanks be to God—through Jesus Christ our Lord!"* followed by the simple confession of our reality: *"So then, I myself in my mind am a slave to God's law, but in the sinful nature a slave to the law of sin."*

I decided to attempt a spiritual experiment. I was going to—no matter how contrary to my mood—begin to thank God for things. At this point in the dark night I was ready to try anything to move a step forward, even if it didn't 'feel' like much. So, I began a very silly process. I thanked God when I woke up in the morning that I had woken up. I thanked him that I had a job on days when I sure didn't feel thankful for my job. I thanked him for mundane things like green lights at an intersection or a good cup of coffee. You get the idea. I was going through the motions…the kind of faith that seems like a waste of time because it doesn't feel real. However, it was all I had at that point. Then, as you may have already guessed, something really strange began to happen. Actual gratitude began to come out of my heart. In this dark night of the soul where everything seemed heavy and miserable, I began to really be grateful for some things. In particular, one night, I was praying for my daughters. I began to reflect on life before them and life since them. Life since has been so much richer. I was overtaken by gratitude flowing from my spirit. "Thank you, Father for giving me my kids. They've really changed my life and blessed me," I prayed. This moment of true gratitude opened the gate for me. I began to thank God for things in a real way. I still thanked him for green lights at times—but I meant it! Gratitude melted something very hard in my heart. Being grateful is so much more than saying 'thank you'. Gratitude is the weapon we need to fight off some serious foes. One of those is selfishness. When you begin to be grateful in your heart you begin to see just how much God does for you, how generous he is in all things. This made me aware of my own selfishness and as I saw it, I did not like it. It allowed me to begin changing that part of my heart that wanted to focus solely on me. Gratitude also shines light on our lives and brings things into a better focus. Without gratitude, I would inflate the things in my life that I saw as negatives until they were so monstrous that they not only angered me, but scared me. I would never have linked gratitude to helping me in this way, but I found that as I was genuinely grateful for things, these negatives deflated to a more realistic status. I was able to look at them and realize that though they were real, they were perhaps not as insurmountable as I had thought. Why does being grateful to God have such an effect on the human heart? I think one reason it is so profound is because at the core of gratitude is one of the most important powers known in the universe: love. We acknowledge God's love for us when we thank him and as we acknowledge that love and realize how deep it is, we are transformed by the immensity of how all-encompassing it is. One of the most powerful moments of gratitude is when in our struggle with Sin we turn to God and say, "Thank you for your mercy." Sin cannot stand against Jesus. When it comes up against him it loses…it deflates. Its power must lessen as Christ's presence increases within our hearts. If you don't want to be grateful, at least be grateful to Jesus for his mercy and forgiveness. This one 'thank you' is enough to change our hearts and minds in incredible ways, leading us to a fuller life wherein we walk in the peace and freedom promised to us by Jesus.

In hard times it can be difficult to be grateful. As I walked in the dark night, that is certainly how I felt, but I persisted. I had become determined to follow Jesus out of this valley and I was certain that in gratitude I'd found a way to begin moving that way. I was looking at part of the bridge I'd been seeking from Romans 7 over to 8. There was yet one more element to that bridge and it turned out it had a lot to do with where I'd begun my journey into the dark night of the soul.

## 4

I own many books. I love to read, and much to my wife's chagrin, I like to keep the books that I've read. Sometimes I peruse my many books and recall how much I enjoyed particular ones. One day as I passed by a stack of books (yes there are spots in my little townhouse where there are simply piles of books resting atop one another) my eye was drawn to one. The title seemed to jump out at me: Paul, the Church and the Spirit of God by Gordon Fee. I'd read it quite some years ago and I recalled how much I'd enjoyed it. I know enough these days to recognize when God is tapping me on the shoulder. So, I picked it up and over the next week or so I reread the book. If you are looking for a book to read about the Holy Spirit that has some solid theology and sheds light on Paul, then I recommend Fee's book. Reading this book caused a major shift within me. For the first time in a long while I began to experience a new thirst for God's presence. In the dark night of the soul we often feel spiritually hungry and thirsty, but find it very difficult to find any satisfaction. This thirst was different. I could sense that there was something here for me that would satisfy my thirst. I spent some time reflecting on this and soon I realized what it was that I desired in my heart.

"Lord," I prayed. "I want to keep this simple. I want to know Holy Spirit for who he is."

I contemplated this further and decided that I needed the simplest prayer possible. Believe it or not it took me two days to come to a wording that I was happy with (if you haven't guessed, I tend to overthink things sometimes). I began to simply pray this prayer: "Holy Spirit, I pray that you would show me your presence." I didn't know what to expect and that was the point of it. I was ready to set aside my preconceived ideas and my previous experiences with him. It was time to clear the stage and give him the freedom to show me who he was in the ways that he wanted to. This was very important to me. There were many good points in Fee's book, but the one that had struck me the most at this time was that Holy Spirit is given to us as a guarantee of the life to come. His presence is a sign that points to Jesus continually. He is the evidence within us that testifies to the reality of Jesus and all that Jesus has accomplished through the cross and the resurrection. What's more, as Fee points out repeatedly in his book, Paul would be completely confused by a Christian living their life without experiencing the Spirit's presence. For him it was so much a part of the Christian life and experience that anything less would have seemed extremely odd. Those who know me well know that I am not unacquainted with the Holy Spirit, but I had reached a new point in my spiritual life that seemed to require a fresh start in my relationship with him. Call it going deeper or moving to a new level if you want, but for me it was time to allow him to reveal himself to me completely on his terms. It seemed I had come full circle. As you will recall, at the outset of this self-reflection my journey into the dark night of the soul began with exactly this same desire and intention, only my focus was on the person of Jesus. Let me quote from above so you don't have to go back: "You know what I want, Lord? I want you to tell me about who you are and what you're like. I want to really know you. So…I invite you to come and sit with me at a table with two chairs, somewhere private. All I want is you, Lord. I just want to hear from you what you say about yourself." Now I was echoing that same desire regarding Holy Spirit. When this began I hadn't yet begun to write this story out, so it wasn't until months later that I saw the connection. There was more than two years between the start of this dark night and my new found thirst to know Holy Spirit in the same way that I had wanted to know Jesus.

  Days flowed into weeks as I faithfully prayed my short, crafted prayer. I prayed it as often as I thought of it. Every time I said the words a hint of anticipation would arise in my heart. For the first time in what seemed like forever, I was beginning to feel life in my spirit. I went back to Romans 7 and 8 and I thought I could see the bridge clearly now. Gratitude was like a key opening the gate and allowing Holy Spirit the freedom to do what he wanted within me on his terms and according to who he is. This was the bridge into the spiritual life Paul describes, which I had been longing for.

  There were no visions, no heavenly visitations, and no supernatural experiences to wow the imagination. Instead small things began to occur within my heart that took me some time to recognize. I would get to the end of a day and upon reflection realize that I had become more patient. "Well how did that happen?" I'd wonder. Holy Spirit would whisper to me, *"That's me—my presence within you."* Another day I'd realize how much my heart had softened: *That's me—my presence within you.* I began to experience what seemed like random moments of inner peace for which I could give no explanation: *That's me—my presence within you.* Times of joy that were entirely new to me: *That's me—my presence within you.* The ability to show love when before I would give way to anger and frustration: *That's me—my presence within you.* I'm sure you get the idea. Galatians 5 speaks of the fruit of the Spirit and I realized that he was quietly working within me and the evidence was in these fruits. It was remarkable to me. For example, I wasn't trying to be more patient, but because of his presence, I was becoming more patient.

I continue to pray this prayer daily and I just might keep it up for the rest of my life. I am learning that Holy Spirit's presence is not only vital to my spiritual life and transformation, but that he takes great joy in his role. My relationship with him has grown in a way that I didn't expect. He is always present with me. I need only turn my heart towards him and I find him immediately there within me, welcoming and full of love. His presence is always full of comfort and strength. He is always at work within me, tinkering away at my heart, poking and prodding at the places there that still need his changing touch. I have grown to trust him more than I did before the dark night began. To use familiar language, I've begun to know him both as friend and counsellor. I realize that there is so much for me to learn about who he is and in some ways I feel like my relationship with him has only just begun. When I was younger, I experienced the presence of Holy Spirit in amazing ways.

Now, I am beginning to *know* him and it leaves me in awe of him.

*

I believe my journey through the dark night of the soul is coming to an end. I'm not quite out of the valley yet, but I'm certainly not down in the mire of the lowest point of the valley anymore. Signs of life have been appearing and I can only hope that as I emerge from the dark night, I will have learned all that Jesus wanted to teach me during this time and that I've been changed in the ways that he has sought to transform me. It may seem odd, but I'm nervous. I've been in the dark night for quite a long time, and though it has been a hard road, it has become home in some ways. Where will my spiritual life go to once Jesus leads me out of the dark night? I have no idea. However, I trust him more now than I did before this road began and I will follow him wherever he wishes to lead me, for I've learned that God loves me. I have no way to tell you how deep that statement goes into my being now. It is the most powerful knowledge in the universe. Nothing can overcome that love.

In closing, I would like to share a concern that has arisen in my heart. When I realized that I'd entered this spiritual season of the dark night, or desert, I had an understanding of what was happening. I've read books that speak of it. I know people that have gone through it. I had the knowledge to at least understand that I'd entered a long process meant to accomplish something. But how many believers aren't aware? How many have felt plunged into this difficult season without knowing what was happening to them? When everything that used to fill them with spiritual energy lost its potency, was their faith seriously wounded? I suspect there are many Christians out there who've entered the dark night of the soul without knowing much about it and have gotten lost there to such a degree that they've given up on their spirituality and are as dry as tinderboxes in their hearts and souls. In the dark night it is easy to feel alone and even abandoned by God, though this isn't the case at all. But if you've never heard of or been taught about what the dark night looks like, you could easily feel that somehow everything had been cut off from you. It is for these people that I share this story of what has happened to me. I can only hope that some will stumble upon it and realize that God loves them and has never abandoned them. In fact, he is calling them to a deeper faith, a faith rooted in who he is. I learned during the dark night of the soul that God is never actually silent. I know some of the classics on this topic might disagree with me, but what I learned was that the ways in which he was speaking had changed. The ways that I was used to hearing him no longer seemed to happen, and that was initially very difficult for me. Yet, slowly I began to hear him anew in ways that were different. I found that in times of deep silence, I would look back and he would show me how he had indeed been speaking, but it was in a place so deep in my heart that I couldn't hear in the ways I was used to.

The dark night of the soul is a hard road to walk. I won't try and make it sound better than it is. However, as I begin my slow ascent out of the valley towards a new season, I want to let you know that it was worth every agonizing step.

ERIC H JANZEN
## Prayer

*Father, I thank you for your immense love. I thank you for loving me so much that you invite me to walk in a truly deep relationship with you. I thank you that even in the midst of my anguish and weakness, you are present. I thank you, Lord Jesus for sitting with me when all I can pray is a groan from my spirit. I thank you that even when I haven't been able to see your footsteps, you've walked and carried me forward with you, for you truly never abandon or give up on us. I pray that you would show me your presence, Holy Spirit. Open my senses—my eyes and my ears—so that I become more sensitive and aware of all that you are doing within me and around me. I want to know you on your terms, Father, Son and Holy Spirit. I lay down my expectations and invite you to show me who you truly are—Amen.*

**Scripture for Reflection:**
Psalm 40
Psalm 42
Psalm 146
Romans 7-8
Hebrews 12

There is a cavern somewhere
Within my heart
Away from the clutching and the grasping
Wherein a lantern glows
With the amber pulsing of the Presence
And the invitation to sit
In a solitary moment awash
With the rays of peace shimmering
In a rare darkness that
Knows nothing of fear
Or angst
Breath leaves lungs
While eyes flutter and close
Lips quiet...
And the feet of my soul
Descend into the cavern
Where a broken heart
Meets a sacred one

## Conclusion

If I was asked to name the central theme weaving its way through all of these reflections, I would probably answer with 'Love'. Yet, that simple word can't convey the fullness of the theme we use it to describe. The longer I walk with Jesus attempting to do so with an open and honest heart without preconceived ideas and expectations, the more I discover that his love is so great it can't be fully described. When words fail, we are left with a deep sense of awe at his love. Those are precious moments of worshipping in spirit and in truth.

I'm not sure that everyone arrives at this kind of shore with God, but I believe we are all invited to come and sit with him on these sands. Again and again, Jesus calls to us with his open hands, filled with his love, grace, and mercy. He calls us to look to him instead of focusing on those things which distract us from this great love he has for us and our neighbors.

Often, when I pray, I find myself saying these words:

*Lord Jesus, I pray you would increase until you fill my vision with just you. I want to know you and you alone. Let everything else and every other voice grow silent in your presence. You are all I want—Amen.*

I leave you with that simple prayer. May your journey be increasingly filled with the presence of the Father, Son and Holy Spirit.

Eric H Janzen

Manufactured by Amazon.ca
Bolton, ON